A Dangerous Experiment

100 Years of Women at the University of Michigan

BY

Dorothy Gies McGuigan

"By many it is regarded as a doubtful experiment, by some as a very dangerous experiment . . . certain to be ruinous to the young ladies who should avail themselves of it . . . and disastrous to the Institution which should carry it out . . . "

—Regents' Report on the Admission of Females, 1858

Center for Continuing Education of Women • Ann Arbor • 1970

Research Assistants: Shirley Davis Schumacher
Linda Walker

Cover Design by Mary Kay Oliver

Printed in the United States of America by
R.W. Patterson Printing Company, Benton Harbor, Michigan

Foreword

If it is true, as more than one historian now avers, that the emancipation of women was the most momentous fact of the nineteenth century, then the hazardous experiment that began when women were admitted to Michigan in 1870 was an event of truly historical significance.

Our book tells the story of women's struggle to win admission to the largest university in the country, of the pioneer women who had the audacity to come to an all-male college, of the obstacles that met them, of what they chose to do with their dearly won educations.

And we close with the question: where are women today in the first great university to open its doors to us? And, perhaps more importantly, where are we not?

Jean W. Campbell
Director
Center for Continuing Education of Women

Table of Contents

Table of Contents

University of Michigan, 1865

1

1870: New Student on Campus

One Law for Man and Woman.
—Bronson Alcott, in Madelon Stockwell's autograph album
February 14, 1870

Little wonder, of course, that when Madelon Stockwell appeared on the campus of the University of Michigan on a snowy day in February of 1870, she was at once the target of curious stares, of pointed fingers and whispered remarks—not only from her thousand or so fellow students, but of the men on the faculty and the people of Ann Arbor.

It was not, moreover, a very friendly curiosity. Indeed her initial reception was as chilly as that raw February day. Her examinations for admission had been, she wrote a friend, "longer and more severe than those given the young men."[1]

When she was called upon to recite for the first time in Professor Martin D'Ooge's Greek class, whether by accident—as she kindly believed later—or out of waggish humor not unstreaked with malice—she had to read aloud from Sophocles' *Antigone* the rebuke of Ismene to her sister:

> It behooves us in the first place to consider this, that we
> are by nature women, so not able to contend with men;
> and in the next place, since we are governed by those
> stronger than we, it behooves us to admit to these things
> and those still more grievous.

As she left campus soon after, she found herself running a gaunt-
let of young men students lined up in force on either side of the
Diagonal Walk "hoping to stare [her] out of countenance."[2]

A student named Vincent Lovell wrote in his diary that week of
the appearance of the "She-sophomore."

In the local newspapers of Ann Arbor and Ypsilanti, Madelon
Stockwell could have read editorials excoriating the Regents for
permitting an experiment "detrimental . . . to the best interests of
the University", accusing the Regents of "floating on the tide of the
radical party," warning that "Delilahism has gained ground, until
free love and woman's rights have prevailed," and indeed that
doomsday was not far off, when all true scholars would have to
leave the University and go abroad for their education.[3]

Years later, looking back, Madelon Stockwell bore no grudges.
The only trace of bitterness in her recollections was of a party she
attended in Ann Arbor "of about two hundred, and not a woman
except the hostess and her daughter spoke to me during the whole
evening."[4]

Two years earlier, in 1868, the first black students, John Summer-
field Davidson and Gabriel Franklin Hargo, had enrolled in Michigan without incident, stirring so little attention that no mention
can be found either in college records nor in the student press.[5]

Yet it is not strange that Madelon Stockwell's appearance, a
lone female figure in bonnet and gloves and trailing skirts—"the
most modest and shy of women," a friend described her,—should
have provoked such curiosity and hostility.[6]

For women in 1870 were as yet many years away from the rights
of citizenship. They could not vote nor hold public office. Whether,
if married, they might or might not control their own property was
still a matter of debate in some states. While Michigan had been
the second state to grant married women such property rights, not
until 1911 would they gain legal control over their own earnings.[7]

As for higher education for women, the question had been con-
troversial for centuries. And the still newer question—whether that
higher education might be side by side with men—had been argued

for nearly twenty years, on the floor of the State Legislature, in the meeting rooms of the faculty and the Regents, in pulpits and in the press—and in kitchens and parlors all over Michigan.

The debate revolved around three main questions: whether the intellect of woman was capable of advanced learning; whether women's physical constitution could stand the rigors of higher education; and whether, in any case, it was both a mistake and a waste to educate women for anything except their proper sphere—and everyone knew what that sphere was.

Diagonal Walk and Old Fence in Winter, 1890.

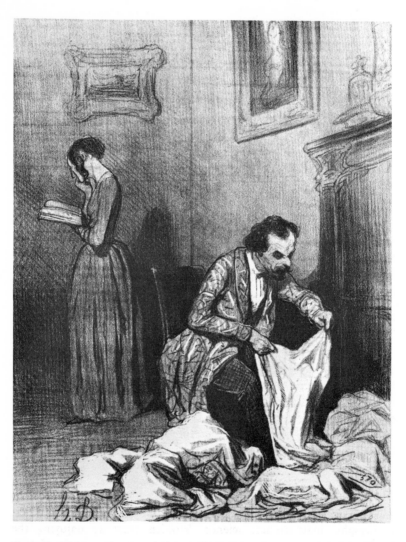

Since Virginie won the seventh honorable mention for poetry from the French Academy, I—captain in the National Guard—have to count the laundry every Saturday and give it to the washerwoman . . . and I do it because otherwise my wife would give me a rough time!

—Honoré Daumier, *The Blue Stockings*

Daumier was among those who satirized literary women in the 1840's in France.

2

Before 1870: Women and History

At least two of those arguments against higher education for women might have been effectively laid to rest had history been more informative about the female sex. But written history itself has been a one-sided affair, often seeming like nothing more than a view of the past through one eye of a pair of binoculars— "a little queer, unreal, lop-sided," says Virginia Woolf, noting that woman "pervades poetry from cover to cover—She is all but absent from history."

And yet we do catch glimpses of her now and again—a letter, a will, even a nursery rhyme—that shed sudden vivid light on what her life must have been. That more women than men read and wrote during the Middle Ages is a strong probability. Women were excluded, of course, from the universities that sprang up during the Middle Ages, for they were semi-monastic foundations, designed primarily to educate young men for the Church. But single women —like single men—could follow a life-time career of higher learning in a convent, perhaps the only instance when society has afforded a high status position to the unmarried woman.

During the Renaissance girls as well as boys studied the classics, philosophy, mathematics, science. Women grew up enjoying the pursuit of higher learning, matched wits with men, as in Castiglione's *The Courtier,* to their mutual pleasure. In Italy women not only studied in the universities but gifted women taught at Bologna and Milan. Laura Bassi, having won a doctorate at twenty-one at Bologna, was appointed in 1732 to a professorship, lectured on Newton's *Optics,* wrote treatises on physics, bore twelve children —whom, we are told, she chose to educate herself.

Women died often in childbirth—but not of learning.

Though women were traditionally excluded from political participation because they could not bear arms, still, as we know, daughters sometimes reigned in place of sons, or mothers for sons; it even happened on occasion that women's negotiating skills were put to use, as at the Ladies' Peace of Cambrai in 1529.

One of the most notable groups of middle class women to find access to the highest scholarship were the women printers, who from the invention of movable type, set, composed, published and sold many of the learned treatises that issued from the early presses. The nuns of the Convent of San Jacopo de Ripoli in Florence were printing even before the turn of the fifteenth century. In the following two centuries some of the finest printed books bore the names of women printers.

In Paris in 1502 Charlotte Guillard began a career that lasted nearly fifty years and brought her Europe-wide renown for her exquisite book-making. In France, in the Lowlands, in Germany, Italy and the British Isles, the wives, daughters and widows of printers worked in the family business and obviously found some way to read and write not only their own language but often Latin, Greek, and Hebrew as well.

That the married professional woman of the twentieth century, juggling the various sectors of her life, is no new phenomenon in history is clearly shown in the lives of these women, many of whom both printed and sold books, managed with credit complex literary estates, continued the process of self-education needed to carry on the business, and meantime reared large families—as their wills clearly show.

Almost the only glimpse of their private lives comes from those wills. Certainly they took time out from business to keep house, for with what scrupulous feminine precision they distribute not only their valuable printing businesses, but their household goods— silver platters and candlesticks, featherbeds, bolsters and sheets, even the "best gowne and frilled petticote." And even in their wills they keep a solicitous maternal eye on their offspring. Joan Wolfe in 1574 leaves an annuity for her son, "provided alwaies that the saide henrye . . . applie his studdye at the universitie." And Joanne Jugge leaves one of her daughters only her "least guilte salte without a cover" because the giddy girl has already required two dowries.[1]

The advent of Luther and the stony Calvinist detour were hardly unmixed blessings to women. As Erik Erikson points out, "Luther provided new elements for the western male's identity; but he contributed only one new feminine identity, the parson's wife."[2] The feminine element vanished from religion with the dethronement of Mary; with the closing of the convents an important avenue of education for girls vanished. Moreover, the old authoritarian and patriarchal concept of the family hardened; to writers of the Puritan mold, such as Sir Thomas Browne, women were simply "formed from the rib of a man and a crooked piece at that." Marriage was the only acceptable occupation for women, and the only suitable education was one which fit them into their predestined place.

A famous seventeenth century educational tract, *The Ladies' Calling*, exhorted women to perfect obedience—first to their fathers, then to their husbands—argued that education would end by unsexing them and making them unfit for their natural vocation. Indeed, wrote the author, the evil consequences were already apparent:

> . . . some men have become effeminate, and some women bold, even swearing and drinking, a prodigious thing in women.[3]

A conspicuous exception to the rigidly defined sexual status quo was the Society of Friends, with its great emphasis on the value of the individual human being. From its founding the Quakers admitted women to equality of membership and favored equal education of the sexes.

The first conception of a women's college came from the pen of an English spinster, Mary Astell; in *A Serious Proposal to the Ladies* in 1695 she proposed an academy of higher learning that would offer women languages, science, philosophy, literature. Mary Astell was not suggesting anything so radical as preparing women for a professional life; she merely claimed that the daughters of English nobility might be better prepared for marriage through the pursuit of advanced studies. Timid though Mary Astell's proposal appears today, her book brought down the wrath of the clergy and the ridicule of society.

Ridicule would prove an effective weapon against any woman's ambition to study or to write. The "philosophical lady" and the "she-clarke" had been the butt of satire in broadsides and on the stage since the early seventeenth century. While Molière ostensibly only pricked the pretentions of pedantic women in his *Les Femmes Savantes,* his play was widely imitated and he added to the opprobrium attached to the term, "learned woman." Not only men writers satirized the learned lady, but such women as Aphra Behn and Susanna Centlivre made fun of her too. The term "blue stocking," originally applied to both men and women in the literary circle of Mrs. Montague in mid-eighteenth century London, came to be entirely derogatory and to apply only to women.

In the latter part of the eighteenth century, two important books appeared that would affect, in differing ways, attitudes toward women for generations.

One was Sir William Blackstone's *Commentaries on the Laws of England* (1765). His chapter entitled "On Husband and Wife" appeared to deny married women any individual existence at all as legal beings. Blackstone wrote:

> the very being or legal existence of the woman is suspended during the marriage . . . A man cannot grant anything to his wife, or enter into covenant with her, for to grant would be to suppose her a separate existence . . [4]

In actual practice equity law often protected married women's property rights. But Blackstone's opinions were highly influential on legal thinking, and his implication that a woman "died civilly" the day she married would provide fuel for women's rights leaders in the years that followed.

And although the Enlightenment and the French Revolution would proclaim the liberty and equality of men, even Rousseau did not consider that women could be included in those terms. In his famous treatise on education, *Emile,* Rousseau delivered his judgment: that girls should be educated at home, by their mothers, in household arts, and in modesty, virtue, obedience; above all, let them avoid the study of philosophy and the arts of the salon.

It took a spirited young Englishwoman, Mary Wollstonecraft, to write a flaming defence of women's right to share fully in the basic principles of the American and the French Revolutions.

The power and logic of her arguments had been wrung out of the anguish of her own life. Daughter of a brutal father who had often beaten his wife and daughters, Mary left home, still in her teens, to make a precarious living from the meager choices offered middle-class girls of that day. Working as a rich woman's companion, organizing and teaching a school for small children, doing translations and adaptations, she lived always on the borderline of bleak poverty.

Stirred by Thomas Paine's tract on the rights of man, Mary Wollstonecraft in 1792 wrote *A Vindication of the Rights of Woman* in the space of six weeks:

> Contending for the rights of woman, my main argument is built on this simple principle, that if she be not prepared by education to become the companion of man, she will stop the progress of knowledge and virtue . . . the love of mankind, from which an orderly train of virtues spring, can only be produced by considering the moral and civil interests of mankind; but the education and situation of woman, at present, shuts her out from such investigations.[5]

Disagreeing with Rousseau, Mary Wollstonecraft declared that her own experience in teaching children showed her that little girls were not born docile and dependent, but were conditioned to be so. She argued not only for better education for women, but for coeducation of the sexes, for training women for useful employment, and for the rearing of women to think and act independently.

It is difficult to believe that her tract, written during the French Revolution, could appear so radical to her contemporaries, but its publication brought down on the author a storm of angry invective; Horace Walpole called her "a hyena in petticoats."

Mary had just begun to write an autobiographical novel called *The Wrongs of Woman* when she died in childbirth, of puerperal fever, in 1797. Her child, Mary Godwin, survived and would grow up to be the wife of Percy Bysshe Shelley.

While Mary Wollstonecraft in England wrote the book that would be a primer of the women's reform movement, across the Atlantic American women too were protesting the exclusion of their sex from participation in what was euphemistically called a free society.

From colonial times women had been an economically precious, desperately needed minority, had been called upon to share physical danger and hardships side by side with men. Especially in the expanding West they enjoyed greater social freedom than women anywhere. But to more than one woman it appeared bitter hypocrisy that a republic forged out of the libertarian, egalitarian principles of the Enlightenment offered those rights only to males.

A few weeks before the Declaration of Independence was written, on March 31, 1776, Abigail Adams was writing to her absent husband, the future President:

> I long to hear that you have declared an independancy—and by the way in the new Code of Laws which I suppose it will be necessary for you to make I desire you would Remember the Laidies, and be more generous and favourable to them than your ancestors. Do not put such unlimited power into the hands of the Husbands. Remember all Men would be tyrants if they could. If perticuliar care and attention is not paid to the Laidies we are determined to foment a Rebelion, and will not hold ourselves bound by any Laws in which we have no voice, or Representation.[6]

John Adams replied:

> As to your extraordinary Code of Laws, I cannot but laugh. We have been told that our Struggle has loosened the bands of Government everywhere. That Children and Apprentices were disobedient—that Schools and Colledges were grown turbulent—that Indians slighted their Guardians and Negroes grew insolent to their Masters. But your Letter was the first Intimation that another Tribe more numerous and powerfull than all the rest were grown discontented. This is rather too coarse a Compliment, but you are so saucy, I won't blot it out. Depend upon it. We know better than to repeal our Masculine systems.

If he thought her proposal for political rights for women ridiculous, John Adams did agree with his wife's complaint about education—up to a point.

A few weeks after her plea for political rights, Abigail wrote to her husband (August 14, 1776):

> If you complain of neglect of Education in sons, what shall I say with regard to daughters, who every day experience the want of it. With regard to the Education of my own children, I find myself soon out of my depth, and destitute and deficient in every part of Education.

And John Adams replied (August 25, 1776):

> Your Sentiments of the Importance of Education in Wo-
> men are exactly agreeable to my own. Yet the Femmes
> Scavans are contemptible Characters.

What most men in that day thought should be women's education may be seen in the address delivered by James Milnor, Esquire, before the graduation audience at the Philadelphia Academy
for Young Ladies in 1809:

> The modesty and amiableness of her character should
> ever be considered by a well-bred woman as ornaments
> of too valuable a description to give place to the affec-
> tation and conceit of scholastic attainments, and it should
> be her constant study to avoid an ostentatious display of
> the decorations of her mind.

Mr. Milnor especially warned against encouraging young ladies

> to attempt the highest flights of scientific attainment,
> not to involve themselves in laborious efforts to become
> acquainted with the dead languages, or familiar with all
> the subtleties of an abstract philosophy.[7]

His basic message came through with crystalline clarity. Young
ladies should not aspire to any other learning than simple matters
of grammar, geography and arithmetic.

A distinctive characteristic of the pro-woman movement as it
developed in the 1840's and '50's in the United States—distinguish-
ing it from movements in England and continental Europe—was its
close correlation with the cause of abolishing chattel slavery.

Although the parallel was certainly a very loose one and applied
only to certain aspects of the problems of two disadvantaged
groups, it is interesting that defenders of slavery, and both defenders and opponents of women's rights saw a parallel between
the position of women in a paternalistic society and that of the
black slave.[8]

In actual fact the women's reform movement was more difficult
and complex. It involved not a sector but the entire population.
It appeared to threaten not only the economy but the structure of
the family, and it threatened to modify the most profound of all

relationships, the sexual. In the life and thought of Victorian America an immense gap existed between the myth of woman as a delicate, fragile, virtually sexless creature, whose sole purpose, nevertheless, was procreation, and the harsh reality: that already thousands of women were at work in the lowest-paid jobs in mill and factory, in domestic service and prostitution, and that women as a whole were denied any opportunity to better their position through higher education and through representation in government.

Among the earliest agitators for women's rights were Sarah and Angelina Grimke', daughters of a wealthy South Carolina plantation owner. In the 1830's the sisters became converts to Quakerism and passionate advocates of abolition.

Angelina Grimke' wrote in 1838:

> The investigation of the rights of the slave has led me to a better understanding of my own. I have found the Anti-Slavery cause to be the high school of morals in our land—the school in which human rights are more fully investigated, and better understood and taught, than in any other.[9]

Angelina and her sister Sarah, who wanted to study law but was barred by her sex, travelled through New England speaking out against slavery, the first women in the United States to speak in public before mixed audiences. Almost the whole New England clergy rose up in horror at the sisters' audacity. The Congregational clergy published a Pastoral Letter taking to task those

> who encourage females to bear an obtrusive and ostentatious part in measures of reform, and countenance any of that sex who so far forget themselves as to itinerate in the character of public lecturers and teachers.[10]

Sarah Grimke' put her sharp logical mind into a series of *Letters on the Condition of Woman and the Equality of the Sexes:*

> I rejoice because I am persuaded that the rights of woman, like the rights of slaves, need only be examined to be understood and asserted, even by some of those who are now endeavoring to smother the irrepressible desire for mental and spiritual freedom which flows in the breast of many who hardly dare to speak their sentiments.[11]

BEFORE 1870: WOMEN AND HISTORY

American women continued to study in that school of human rights of which Angelina Grimke' had spoken. Excluded from joining the American Anti-Slavery Society, women abolitionists had to form an organization of their own, the National Female Anti-Slavery Society. With or without the Constitution to back them, American women began to enter the public arena and to study the art of political maneuver.

In June, 1840, a young honeymooning couple, Henry and Elizabeth Cady Stanton, both deeply involved in the anti-slavery cause, sailed for England to take part in a World Anti-Slavery Convention. For an entire day English and American male delegates argued about seating women at the convention. In the end the women delegates were barred. Smoldering with anger and resentment, they sat for twelve days behind a curtained-off partition and listened to the all-male delegation discuss plans for their cause.

Eight years later, in July of 1848, two of the women barred from that anti-slavery convention, Elizabeth Cady Stanton and Lucretia Mott, called a meeting in Seneca Falls, New York, "to discuss the social, civil, and religious rights of women." Several hundred men and women appeared, and because not one of the women present had the courage or the experience to chair the meeting, Lucretia's husband, James Mott, presided. A Declaration of Sentiments, paraphrasing the Declaration of Independence, listed some eighteen grievances of woman against man:

> He has denied her the facilities for obtaining a thorough education, all colleges being closed to her. He has usurped the prerogative of Jehovah himself, claiming it as his right to assign for her a sphere of action, when that belongs to her conscience and to her God . . . He has endeavored in every way that he could, to destroy her confidence in her own powers, to lessen her self-respect, and to make her willing to lead a dependent and abject life.

The Declaration ended with a ringing demand that women

> have immediate admission to all the rights and privileges which belong to them as citizens of the United States.[12]

Twelve resolutions in line with the Declaration quickly passed; only the resolution claiming the right of franchise for women met with difficulty, but it too passed, thanks to the support of the black abolitionist and ex-slave, Frederick Douglass.

Response to the Declaration of Sentiments was immediate; such ridicule and derision were heaped on the men who had been courageous enough to sign the women's document that a number withdrew their signatures.

The New York Herald reflected the general tone of the press:

> How did woman first become subject to man as she now is all over the world? By her nature, her sex, just as the negro is and always will be, to the end of time, inferior to the white race, and, therefore, doomed to subjection; but happier than she would be in any other condition, just because it is the law of her nature.[13]

—Here we are meeting together to write the first number of our journal, *Le Sans Culotte littéraire*. What shall we start off complaining about?
—To begin with . . . let's complain about everything!
—Honoré Daumier, The Blue Stockings

Ridicule was an effective weapon against women's literary ambitions.

3

A Dangerous Experiment Begins

It was against this background in the 1850's—the rising momentum of the anti-slavery movement and the first agitation of woman's rights activists--that the debate over whether the University of Michigan should be opened to women began.

In Michigan boys and girls had always gone to grade school together, as they had in other parts of the country; simple economy dictated it. More often than not they had gone on together to the high schools, academies and seminaries. Girls had even been admitted to the University's "branches"—preparatory schools set up in towns throughout the state to ready students for the University, since the high schools were by no means of even quality.

Now families with daughters and no sons, or families with daughters as well as sons, began to wonder why, if they paid taxes, their daughters might not go on to the publicly-supported University.

The original statute of the University establishing it in 1837 simply declared that "the University shall be open *to all persons* who possess the requisite literary and moral qualifications."

A few colleges had accepted women in their classes from their founding—notably Oberlin and Antioch in Ohio, Hillsdale in Michigan, the University of Desaret in Utah, and the University of Iowa. And a few women's colleges had already been chartered; Georgia Female College and Mary Sharp College in Tennessee were probably the first.

The first salvo of the battle over coeducation at Michigan was fired in May of 1855, when the liberal-minded State Teachers'

Association held their annual meeting in Ann Arbor, "the most interesting and important ever held by this body." Accounts of the lively debates at that meeting—which counted many women secondary school teachers among its members—were carried in *The Detroit Tribune* and in *The Michigan Argus*.[1]

Professor D. Putnam of Kalamazoo presented all the arguments against coeducation, which he proceeded to refute one by one, concluding with a ringing recommendation that "the system . . . be allowed to have a fair and impartial trial in the highest institution of the State," namely at the University.

Nearly all the speakers who followed Putnam favored the admission of women to the University.

University of Michigan Professor Erastus Haven, who would later become President, claimed long after in his autobiography that he had at this early date supported coeducation:

> So far as I know [he wrote of the Teachers' Convention debate] the subject had not been suggested before. It was considered wild and insane. Not a member of either Faculty approved it, but usually it was regarded as a rather dangerous joke on my part.[2]

In actual fact, according to the report of the proceedings, Haven talked all around the point:

> "If the young women of the country were rising *en masse,* and demanding a college education, why do they not go to [Antioch, Oberlin] where the doors are open? It would not seem that there was so great a demand after all."[3]

Furthermore, he said:

> "If we educate mind simply as mind, this would be right. But if our Colleges in their course of education, look to the preparation of young men for the profession of law, medicine and theology, then women would be necessarily excluded, as she would not choose to follow these professions."[4]

What Haven really favored, both at the Teachers' Conference and later as President of the University, was not the admission of women on an equal basis, but rather a separate and not necessarily equal facility: "a Female Seminary . . . right across the street from our State University."[5]

On the final day of their meeting the state teachers did adopt a resolution "that the coeducation of the sexes is in accordance with true philosophy, and is practically expedient."[6]

If any women applied for admission to the University in the early 1850's, no record remains.

But in March of 1858, according to the Regents' Proceedings, a Miss Sarah Burger of Ann Arbor wrote the Board, informing them that "a class of twelve young ladies would present themselves for admission as students in June next." The Regents hastily tabled that letter, as if it were a combustible substance.[7]

When the Regents met next, at Commencement time in June, one of the chief problems on the agenda was to act on the applications now in hand of Misses Sarah J. Burger and Harriet Ada Patton, of Ann Arbor, and of Miss Augusta J. Chapin of Lansing.

The Regents applied that classical device for handling knotty problems: a committee was appointed to study the matter, and report back in two days.

The next day, June 23, was Commencement—and Commencement in that day was a ceremony designed to be remembered all one's life. Attendance of graduates was compulsory; the solemn procession formed at 9 o'clock in the morning in 94° heat, and marched to the newly-built high school: the Governor, the State Superintendent of Public Instruction and the President of the University, the Board of Visitors, the Board of Regents, the entire faculty, the graduating class, and finally any students who wanted to participate. According to the *Detroit Free Press* reporter, who followed the events of those three days closely, the high school auditorium was jammed to capacity, the ceremony itself took eleven long hours in scorching heat and included no fewer than 13 full-length orations by members of the graduating class including one in Greek and one in Latin, a speech by President Henry P. Tappan, an address by an honored alumnus, and the conferring of degrees. In the evening the President held a levee at his house "for faculty, Regents, alumni and friends."[8]

Exactly when the committee deliberated on the admission of women is not clear, but their report was ready the following morning of June 24 when the Regents again met. Two of the three members declared themselves in favor of admitting women; one member, Benjamin Baxter, former principal of the University's Tecumseh branch, dissented.

"Active and stormy session," the *Free Press* reported of the bitter argument that ensued. No doubt everyone was worn out by Commencement, but President Tappan was not too exhausted to oppose the admission of women with all the force he could muster —and even to take on the governor of the state. Governor Bingham had been invited to give his views on the subject and declared himself "favoring the admission of the ladies"; apparently he added a few remarks about the high-handed and authoritative stance the President and the faculty were taking. President Tappan replied saying "he should call on the Governor to sustain certain charges made by him in the course of his remarks against the University." Tappan then proceeded with all the arguments at his command to persuade the Board to postpone a decision.

He knew that his faculty, almost to a man, bitterly opposed opening the doors to women.

And he himself, who had set about remodelling Michigan along the lines of the German universities, viewed the admission of women as an unbearable threat to his whole concept of what a university should be.

A few years later, when he was no longer President and in self-exile in Europe, Tappan wrote his friend, German Professor E. P. Evans (1867):

> After [the admission of women] no advancement is possible . . . The standard of education must now be accommodated to the wants of girls who finish their education at 16—20, very properly, in order to get married, at the very age when young men begin their education.[9]

Tappan harked back to the anxieties expressed in the seventeenth-century pamphlet, *The Ladies Calling:*

> I sometimes fear we shall have no more women in America. If the Women's Rights sect triumphs, women will try to do the work of men—they will cease to be women while they will fail to become men—they will be something mongrel, hermaphroditic. The men will lose as the women advance, we shall have a community of *defeminated* women and *demasculated* men. When we attempt to disturb God's order we produce monstrosities.

The afternoon of June 24, 1858, ended with the question re-committed to the same committee for study over the summer. In the meantime that afternoon, "a petition from some young ladies of Lansing asking admission as students was received and referred to the committee on the subject." [10]

On September 28, 1858, the Regents again gathered in Ann Arbor, but they did not reach the matter of women until their second day of business. After a favorable vote had been taken to appropriate $12.63 to buy twenty feet of Atlantic Cable for the University Museum, Regent McIntyre rose to read aloud his 14-page report, "On the Admission of Females," which would decide whether Sarah Burger and the other applicants would be the first women at Michigan. [11]

The report began by pointing out that the State Superintendent of Public Instruction earnestly advocated the right of women to a university education, on the ground that the founding statute open-ed the University "to all *persons* resident of this State," and claim-ing that women are comprised in that definition, "person."

It was a crucial point. In Blackstone it was implicit that women were not "persons." A few years hence, in June of 1873, soon after women were admitted to the University, a presiding judge in Rochester, New York, would agree with Blackstone, that women were not "persons" and therefore were excluded from voting under the Fourteenth Amendment.

The Regents of the University, however, in 1858 were willing to concede generously that in one sense at least ladies might be con-sidered persons. But since certain persons could in any case be barred from the University—such as, for example, "immoral per-sons"—then it followed that the Regents might exclude any persons "whose presence would detract from the character of the Institu-tion, or prevent it from attaining to the proper rank of a Univer-sity."

The fact that coeducation existed in the primary and secondary schools of the state was dismissed as a simple matter of economy. For the same practical reason, the report pointed out, women were admitted to the State Normal School: it was cheaper to hire them as teachers.

However, the report continued, no university had ever attempted to educate both sexes together: ". . . it would be a misapplication of the funds of the University to appropriate them to the education of women."

Now came the overwhelming evidence.

The committee had written during the summer to leading educators all over the country, asking their opinion on the question of coeducating the sexes. It need hardly be said that no women were consulted; such noted educators as Catherine Beecher, Emma Willard were passed over, for this was a decision to be made by men only.

The replies were, on the whole, scarcely astonishing.

President Woolsey of Yale declared that he "is averse to mingling the sexes in any place of education above the school for the elements." For, he adds, "Of what use degrees are to be to girls I don't see, unless they addict themselves to professional life, and I should expect the introduction of such a plan would be met with ridicule."

President Walker of Harvard averred that "there is an immense preponderance of enlightened public opinion against this experiment,"—in which opinion he entirely concurred, and that "its decision must turn in no small measure, on the question whether we propose to educate females for public or private life."

Dr. Nott of Union College was certain the whole matter had "already been decided by the common consent of mankind . . . A difference of sex and of destination through the entire life has in the judgment of mankind been thought to require a difference in the distinctive attributes to be called into exercise . . . Delicacy of sentiment, a feeling of dependence and shrinking from the public view, are attributes sought for in the one sex, in the other decision of character, self-reliance, a feeling of personal independence, and a willingness to meet opposition and encounter difficulties . . . " He could not see how they could be educated together "without endangering alike their virtue and their happiness."

And finally Regent McIntyre read aloud letters from the presidents of two colleges where coeducation had actually been tried: Oberlin and Antioch.

Horace Mann, president of Antioch, had watched the experiment closely for five years. His reply could scarcely have been more cautious:

> The advantages of a joint education are *very great*. The dangers of it are *terrible*. Unless those dangers can be excluded with a degree of probability *amounting almost to certainty,* I must say that I should rather forego the advantages than incur the dangers.

Mann then proceeded to name the grave dangers that lay in wait for the unwary who tried the experiment:

> These dangers consist in their opportunities for association together *without supervision,* or *privately* . . . If, for instance, women students must be permitted in a city like yours to board promiscuously among the inhabitants, I should prefer that the young women of the age should lose the advantages of an education rather than incur the moral danger of obtaining it in that way.

Mann suggested the Regents ask themselves such questions as:

> Can you make yourselves secure against *clandestine* meetings [of the sexes]? And also against clandestine correspondence—reasonably so, for absolute security is impossible. Are your President and Faculty in a state of mind to exercise vigilance over the girls committed to their care as conscientiously as they would over their own daughters or sisters?

If Horace Mann's letter did not thoroughly dampen any enthusiasm for coeducation among the Regents, the letter from President C. G. Finney of Oberlin most certainly did:

> With us the results are quite satisfactory and even, we think, admirable. You will need a wise and pious matron with such lady assistants as to keep up sufficient supervision. You will need a powerful religious influence to act upon the whole mass of students. You will need a surrounding community who are united in sustaining the regulations and laws of the University in their details, so far as the moral conduct of the young is concerned.

The gentlemen listening to these grave words must surely have blanched.

Some years before, dormitories for men had been abolished in order to reduce the chores of discipline and regulation. Even so, there had been quite enough troublesome problems involving young male students—and frequently friction between town and gown; the thought of maintaining the kind of monastic atmosphere President Finney described at Oberlin was enough to shake the resolution of the staunchest defender of coeducation—and there were none of these in any case on the Board of Regents.

The Free Press summarized the committee's findings on the probable results of admitting women:

> It would tend to unwoman the woman and unman the man—it would tend to produce confusion, and all confusion produces corruption.[12]

In conclusion the committee, while protesting they were certain the application of the young ladies for admission had nothing to do with the unpopular woman's rights movement, managed to leave a strong impression that in fact these applications very likely did. In a final paragraph they tossed in the hair-raising phrase "Free Love," a phrase to frighten any good Victorian family man concerned with upholding honor, purity and motherhood:

> We give no heed to those who attempt to connect or identify the application of the young ladies which we are now considering with the political or social movements known as "Women's Rights," "Free Love," etc. etc. This application has no such connection in our minds, and we would not have the question prejudiced or the request of these young ladies spurned because some persons who advocate the Free Love movement or attend Women's Rights conventions may also advocate the coeducation of the sexes.[13]

In view of all the dangers involved, it was obviously inexpedient to admit young ladies to attend the University. A suggestion was made that perhaps at some future date, some suitable provision might be made for their further education—a female seminary, no doubt, that would educate young ladies, as Dr. Nott advised, for their special sphere in life.

The findings of the University Board of Regents on the question of coeducation were duly published. The problem did not, however, go away.

In June of the following year, 1859, a petition signed by 1,476 citizens of the state was presented to the Regents, pleading that women be admitted.[14]   .

And apparently not at all dashed by the tone of negative finality in that Regents' report, Sarah J. Burger of Ann Arbor again asked to be admitted, along with three other young ladies.

The Regents' response was to appropriate money to have 2,000 copies of their report printed and circulated throughout the State.

A DANGEROUS EXPERIMENT BEGINS

The next year the Civil War broke out. For the moment the question of admitting women was laid aside.

As for those young women who had been so audacious as to apply to an all-male university, the facts are meager, but they suggest interesting portraits of all three.

None of them gave up the idea of higher education, after the doors of the University had slammed in their faces. Two of the three waited patiently and determinedly for many years to win University of Michigan degrees.

Harriet Ada Patton was eighteen years old, newly graduated from Ann Arbor's Union High School when she applied in 1858. Eventually in 1872 she became the second woman to receive a law degree from the University.

Augusta Chapin of Lansing, turned down by the Regents, went to Olivet College, eventually earned one of the coveted early advanced degrees the University granted: a Master of Arts in 1884. She was the first woman in the United States to hold a Doctor of Divinity degree, from Lombard College a few years later. Ordained a minister of the Universalist Church, she held pastorates in Michigan and other states, served as extension lecturer at the University of Chicago, was a leader in the World Parliament of Religions, and still an active pastor in Mount Vernon, New York, when she died there in 1905.

The very first applicant of all had been Sarah Burger of Ann Arbor. According to her biographer, her double rebuff by the University led to her pioneering in the cause of women's rights.

Sarah Burger was, apparently, highly intelligent, "head and shoulders above others in her class," according to friends; she was also pretty—to judge from the faded newspaper clipping in her obituary file—and energetic and determined.

Turned down twice by the Regents, she attended Ypsilanti State Normal School. In 1863 she married Ozora Stearns, a promising young lawyer, serving then in the Union Army as colonel of the 39th U.S. Colored Infantry. Stearns had received his B.S. degree from Michigan in 1858 at the very Commencement when the Regents were pondering Sarah Burger's admission; two years later he earned his law degree. While her husband was at the front, Sarah Burger Stearns travelled through Michigan and adjoining states lecturing to raise money for food, clothing, hospital supplies for the Union Army. An editor of the day commented on her successful public appearances that she had proved it "possible for a lady to speak effectively to a promiscuous audience . . . without stepping out of her true sphere, or compromising her dignity and modesty as a woman."[15]

After the war was over, the young couple settled in Minnesota, where Stearns rose quickly to prominence, elected first to the U.S. Senate from Minnesota, then to district judge. Sarah Stearns wrote and lectured throughout the remaining years of the century in favor of higher education for women. Both she and her husband worked for women's suffrage; Sarah Stearns served as president of the Minnesota Woman's Suffrage Association, and national vice-president of the organization. Mother of three children, she took an interest in numerous social welfare problems, founded a home for destitute women and children in Duluth, and served for several years on the Duluth school board.

Though for a long time she was lost to University of Michigan history, Sarah Burger Stearns believed that her own frustrated attempt to enter had helped speed the acceptance of women students.[16]

In Michigan meanwhile, during the later 1850's and 1860's, the cause of higher education for women had won strong adherents. Among the most remarkable was a Kalamazoo couple, James Andrus Stone and his wife, Lucinda Hinsdale Stone, who had come from the East to take charge of the University's branch school in Kalamazoo. Dedicated teachers and effective public speakers, the Stones were energetic advocates of coeducation; their speeches and writings were very influential in prying open the University's doors to women.

Lucinda Stone had been born in Hinesburg, Vermont, in 1814, youngest of twelve children in one of those huge, unplanned nineteenth-century families.

"I think I was not a very welcome child!" she remarked later. "I used sometimes to wish that I might die, because I thought nobody loved me; but this drove me to my books, and I lived with my books as far back as I can remember."[17]

A bright ambitious girl, Lucinda studied alongside the boys of her town in the college-preparatory curriculum of the local academy —and watched them go off to colleges whose doors were irrevocably closed to her. One day she remarked out loud,

"Oh, I wish I could go to college." The remark brought

down upon me such a deluge of ridicule that I literally
wet my couch with tears over it for many a night . . . Our
postmaster, a narrowminded man, handed my name
about with all kinds of opprobrium in our little village
postoffice, proposing that the citizens of the town petition the Vermont Legislature, then in session, to open
the doors of the state university to "that aspiring young
woman who wanted to go to college." . . . I doubt if I
ever cried so much over any *faux pas* I ever made, or
felt so hurt by the innocent expression of any wish.

Instead of going to college Lucinda went to Natchez, Mississippi,
to teach the children of a wealthy planter. That first-hand view of
slavery was a grimly educational experience that left a deep mark
on her for the rest of her life. Vividly she remembered her first
sight of a slave auction:

A girl stood upon the block. The auctioneer was show-
ing off her good points, making her open her mouth to
show her teeth, use her limbs in various antics to test
her agility, while he chuckled, wheedled, scolded and
threatened . . . It seems strange to me now that I could
have lived through such a scene, but I am not the same
person or being now as then, else I could not have borne
it.

When she returned north a little later and married a Baptist
clergyman, James Stone, and eventually moved to Kalamazoo, the
young couple were both deeply committed to the abolition movement.

In the Kalamazoo branch school, which prepared for the University, Lucinda Stone was principal of the ladies' department:

. . . in my classes, from the first, there were about an
equal number of young men and young women studying
beautifully together, the girls always keeping up fully
with the boys until the boys went to the University and
the girls were supposed to consider their education finished, though I guarded well against the formation of
any such conclusion as that, for my teaching was that
their real education, when they left school, was but
begun, and the question often pressed itself upon me,
why should coeducation stop here, just at the door of
the University? Were not girls, women, mothers, who
certainly were to be the educators of their sons, as much
in need of higher education as boys, men, fathers, who
were expected to lead a life of business, were?[18]

As the University withdrew financial support from its branch schools, the Kalamazoo branch became Kalamazoo College, and Mrs. Stone continued as principal of the ladies' department. Among her outstanding students for a time was the daughter of a former Albion professor, Madelon Stockwell.

During the decade of the 1860's the Stones continued to urge the opening of Michigan University to women. Dr. Stone called on President Henry Tappan to try to persuade him—in vain; he had more luck with the State Legislature in Lansing, where he delivered an address on the subject.

But the Stones' most effective convert was the newly-elected Regent, George Willard, rector of the Episcopal Church in Kalamazoo and Latin professor at Kalamazoo College. They convinced him that nothing in the law prevented women from entering the University, that only prejudice and injustice stood in their way.

Meantime, three or four professors within the University had been won over, not only to the cause of women's rights, but to coeducation as well. It took courage for a woman to espouse the unpopular cause of feminism in the nineteenth century; no doubt it took even more courage for the men who supported it.

Geology Professor Alexander Winchell had listened to the debate at the Teachers' Conference in Ann Arbor in 1855, and since that time he had pondered the inequality of the sexes. In January of 1866—three years before John Stuart Mill published his landmark essay on "The Subjection of Women,"—Winchell wrote in his diary:

> 23 Jan. Looking up facts for an essay on Woman. Commenced essay.
> 24 Jan. Worked all day at essay on Woman.
> 26 Jan. Worked all day at essay on Woman. Read it at Senate Social in evening.1¾ hours long—excited a discussion which lasted till meeting broke up.[19]

Winchell's essay—all 66 pages of it—"Woman—Her Actual Place and her Rightful Place," is a remarkable document. Reviewing the position of women in all ages and in many nations and drawing on dozens of writers from Thucydides to Shakespeare, Winchell drew a detailed picture of men's attitudes toward women, as contrasted to the actual capacities for achievement that women had shown. He wrote:

> Physical prowess only has secured and preserved to man

the dominant place in the family, in society, in education, in political influence. The present age is dwarfing female faculties and narrowing female privileges to a more fearful extent than any other since medieval times . . . I have long been growing into the conviction that we are consenting to a wrong.[20]

He concluded by demanding that women henceforth be given full participation in society—in property rights, in voting, in holding office, in educational privileges.

Another supporter of women's rights—including that of coeducation—was James Robinson Boise, Professor of Greek in the University. Boise was the only member of the University faculty who went on record with the Regents in 1858 as favoring the admission of women: "No reason urged against admission of ladies is sufficient for its denial." He was also father of a bright young daughter, Alice, who graduated from the Union High School in Ann Arbor in 1866.

Years after, Alice Boise recalled the evening of the last public oral examination in Greek—an event of some note in the academic community of Ann Arbor. Alice had acquitted herself brilliantly, and after the examination was finished, stood by while her father chatted with her Greek teacher, and with the President of the University, Erastus Haven, who had a son in Alice's class.

Suddenly my father laid one hand upon the shoulder of young Haven, and one upon me; and gazing earnestly at Dr. Haven, said in impassioned tones, "And your son can go on; but my daughter cannot!"[21]

Boise considered sending Alice to the recently-opened Vassar College, but he learned that the Greek department was far inferior to Michigan's. The autumn after her high school graduation, Alice began to attend her father's Greek class in the University, and a little later was permitted by two other professors to attend their classes. Whether she had or did not have any official sanction to audit is not clear; certainly she was not enrolled as a student.

Here is Alice's recollection of her timid entry into that fearsome all-male world of the campus in 1866:

When in September I went to the college where no woman's foot was known, I stole hurriedly from the back door, ran down path and hillside in trembling alarm. In

> a little room beside my father's classroom, I left my
> shawl and my hat, and waited for the roar of the advanc-
> ing tread of my dreaded classmates. The door opened.
> They entered. Save for a little murmur they were silent.
> The question [of the admission of women] began to
> be earnestly discussed . . . Could women succeed in the
> difficult college studies? Had they the physical strength
> to endure them? And I studied! Perhaps I had not real-
> ized until then that I was representing my sex. Yes, I
> was not studying for myself alone. Surely I must not fail!

Alice's attendance at University classes was no secret, and was duly reported in *The Detroit Post,* where it may have added fuel to the coeducation controversy. In any case the Boises departed the following year for the University of Chicago, where Alice was again admitted to classes on an informal basis.

Gradually opinion was swinging in the direction of the admission of women. At least some university students favored the change, for both student periodicals, *The Chronicle* and *The Oracle,* editor-ialized on the subject, *The Chronicle* suggesting that perhaps the presence of ladies would make the students "less boorish in their manners and less profane in their conversation."[22]

In the spring of 1867 the State Legislature adopted a joint reso-lution declaring that

> the high objects for which the University of Michigan
> was organized will never be fully attained until women
> are admitted to all its rights and privileges.[23]

But the majority of the faculty remained adamantly opposed, and so did President Haven. They felt certain that the admission of women would lower the reputation of the University, based on the assumption of women's mental inferiority. The viewpoint had been succinctly expressed in an article in *The Saturday Review* (1860):

> The great argument against the existence of the equality
> of intellect in women is, that it does not exist. If that
> does not satisfy a female philosopher we have no better
> to find.[24]

When Regent Willard, the Stones' friend, raised the question at the next Regents' meeting, whether women might not be admitted under the admission regulations "on the same conditions and with the same requirements as demanded for men," he got nowhere at all.[25]

Haven, who later claimed that he had favored coeducation all along, equivocated on the subject. In his annual report for that year—1867—he recommended that no change in the admission policy be made, proposing instead a "State College for Young Ladies."

He called the idea of coeducation "a radical revolution," and expounded again on its dangers. "Youth is a transitional period, when passion is strong and restraint is feeble"—and he repeated again the main drift of the Regents' report of 1858.[26]

Dr. Stone, now editor of *The Kalamazoo Telegraph,* continued his spirited defense of coeducation and roundly criticized Haven's scheme for a segregated women's college.

In the end the economics of the whole thing forced the decision.

It was simply cheaper to educate women—if they insisted on education—along with men at the state-supported University. The Legislature knew its taxpayers—they would not consent to ante up another fraction of a mill to build the female seminary that Haven envisioned.

In the autumn of 1868 Haven capitulated—at least so far as to agree that "it is simply wrong" to deny women the use of publicly-supported facilities such as libraries, museums, laboratories. He recommended that Michigan should allow the instruction of women at the University on the same conditions as men. At the end of the year, in June of 1869, wearied no doubt by the problems with which he had had to deal, and with criticisms of his policies, Haven resigned.

With the faculty still opposed to admitting women, the Regents held out stubbornly as long as they could. In April of 1869, on the heels of a resolution by the Legislature favoring the admission of women, Regent Willard introduced a resolution into the Board of Regents permitting them to enter; the resolution was again tabled.

Not until the following January of 1870, when two new members took office on the Board, did the Regents finally take the fatal step.

Regent Willard again introduced his resolution to admit women. Even at the zero hour the Board could not make up their minds. The resolution was tabled; it took a second motion on Willard's part to remove it from the table, and yet another vote to prevent its again being tabled. Finally the resolution was voted on, finally it passed—with a single dissenting vote.[27]

Lucinda Stone happened to be in Ann Arbor and heard at once of the successful outcome. She returned to Kalamazoo post-haste to bring the news to Madelon Stockwell. A few days later Acting President Frieze gave Madelon Stockwell permission to try the entrance examinations; to her joyful surprise she was admitted to the sophomore class.

The admission of women to the University was indeed a historic step, and by and large the American press recognized it as such. It was not the first college to admit women—Oberlin had done so since 1837; nor was it the first state university to do so: Iowa, Wisconsin, Kansas, Indiana, Minnesota and Missouri had all preceded Michigan.

But Michigan was the largest university in the country and had by far the greatest prestige of any college west of New England. *Godey's Lady's Book,* of course, applauded heartily, remarking that the time had passed for "the Oriental system of separating the sexes."[28]

The Cleveland Leader called it "the first large and really first-class institution which has taken the step."

The New York Times said carefully, "Harvard and Yale, which have so long hesitated on the brink, will have an opportunity to observe the effect on those who have plunged boldly in." Harvard and Yale would remain poised on that brink for the better part of a century.

4

Pioneer Women at Michigan University

You would be amused to see how the people in town regard us; for I never go on the street without hearing some such remark as, "See, there is one of them; look at her!" This will all change in time; but it makes it hard for the pioneers who have to bear the brunt of the battle.[1]

—San Louie Anderson, '75

In the September following Madelon Stockwell's admission as a student in the University, 33 more women enrolled; 13 joined her in the Literary Department, 18 were admitted to study medicine, and two into law. They made up just 3 percent of the enrollment.

How did they appear to the University community, those early invaders of the all-male fraternity of the campus? And how did the University appear to them, now that they had won their way into classrooms and lecture halls?

They had to possess exceptional ability, exceptional motivation, for all of them remembered meeting discrimination and prejudice in the first years.

Even to reach college, most had to overcome far greater obstacles than their brothers. To begin with, sons usually had first claim on any available money for education. To persuade her parents to allow her to come to the University, Alice Freeman Palmer had to promise

1870: "Cricket was still played on the muddy lane of State Street between the passing buggies and wagons."

Along the Diagonal Walk young men lined up to stare the first woman student "out of countenance." In the background: tall-domed University Hall, finest of campus buildings.

Madelon Stockwell, first woman admitted: "the target of curious stares, of pointed fingers and whispered remarks." Here she is, many years after, posed at a class reunion.

From the 1840's on, at the University's branch schools, like this one in Kalamazoo, girls as well as boys could prepare for—but never enter—the University.

Lucinda Hinsdale Stone. Mrs. Stone and her husband taught at the Kalamazoo Branch, persuaded a key Regent to support the admission of women to the University.

Acting President Henry Frieze agreed to admit the first women in 1870.

James Burrill Angell, Michigan's third President, staunch defender of higher education for women, took the stigma out of the word "coeducation."

Alice Freeman Palmer, '76, became President of Wellesley College. "Alice knew everybody on campus!"

Olive San Louie Anderson, '75, author. The heroine of her novel of college life at Michigan burned her corsets as a gesture of emancipation.

Lucy Maynard Salmon, '76, scholar and historian, founded the "Q.C.'s", first women's club on campus.

Octavia Bates, '77 (left), with staff of *The Oracle,* sophomore annual, became a lawyer, active in women's causes, took tea with Queen Victoria, left a bundle of money to the University.

Annie Peck, '78, "Queen of the Climbers," gave up school teaching to climb mountains, the higher the better.

Scene in the old library, 1870's.

Coed room: Mabel Joy Livingstone, '01.

that she would not marry until she had paid her younger brother's way through medical school; she kept her promise.

Daughters too were viewed as having heavier obligations to their families than sons; in the large extended families of Victorian days, it was usually an older daughter who had the care of younger children, and perhaps an aged relative or two.

And parents of daughters viewed with apprehension all the dangers thought to be lying in wait for young ladies in the jungle of a coeducational college.

The townspeople of Ann Arbor, probably no different from the townspeople of any other small parochial community, regarded the women students with coldness and at times outright hostility. For these young women were doing a highly unconventional thing: they were entering a male preserve without a cordial invitation.

Two of the first women students, Lucy Maynard Salmon and Louise Hall, walked the streets of the town for three days trying to find a landlady willing to rent them a room. Caroline Hubbard Kleinstueck remembered:

> Whether they thought we were deaf or that it didn't matter how rude they were to such freaks, the words, "There's a University girl" were heard by us on every hand—at lectures, in the streets, and even at church . . . The antagonism of the townspeople was in some ways harder to bear than that of the few students who did protest.[2]

Even at church they were shunned; long after women on campus were a reality, some of the local clergymen were preaching sermons on the evils of coeducation. One of the first women students rented a pew in a local church and attended services every Sunday for a year, the only person to speak to her was the man who collected pew fees.

Before long faculty and students on campus for the most part accepted the women and behaved with consideration and kindness. There were a few hold-outs, such as the instructor who continued to address his class of mixed men and women as "Gentlemen"; when he called on a woman student he called her "Mr. so-and-so," just as if he were still teaching an all-male class.

And some professors had their little jokes, such as the one recounted in the student *Chronicle* soon after Madelon Stockwell's arrival:

A dog had wandered into a classroom, and a couple of
students rose to remove it. The professor stopped them.
"That dog," he said, "is a resident of Michigan. Don't
you know we now recognize the right of every resident
of the state to enjoy the privileges afforded by the University?"[3]

Others were as patronizing as the distinguished professor of law,
Judge Thomas M. Cooley, who wrote to President Andrew White
of Cornell in 1871:

The admission of Women to our classes has scarcely
caused a ripple on the surface of University matters. The
number who come is small, and for the most part of the
unlovely class, some of them afford the boys some
amusement; the strongerminded seize upon the opportunity for a little glorification over the advancement of
"the cause", but things in college move along as before,
and from the moment the thing became an accomplished
fact, it has been to everyone here a matter, I may almost
say, of entire indifference.[4]

The Michigan Argus, which had fought the admission of women
and favored a separate female seminary as President Haven recommended, talked of

the hungry and famished young ladies of the State . . .
bearing down upon the University, Assyrian fashion
   ". . . like the wolf on the fold,
   Their cohorts all gleaming with purple and gold."

The *Argus* writer feared the women students would soon be
demanding

—the women have given over *asking*—for a little piano
and guitar with vocal accompaniment; a little pencil-
sketching, water-coloring and oil-daubing; light gym-
nastics and calisthenics, with all the accomplishments
of a modern belle; the *demand* to be backed by suscept-
ible legislators who never do anything for the University
except to meddle with it—then will the dangerous rocks
show just beneath the water, and the University begin
to scrape her bottom . . .

He believed the young ladies would also insist upon courses on
the chemical analysis of beef, mutton, tea and coffee, on canning,

and, perhaps, a model kitchen might be attached, under the supervision of some feminine BLOT, and a nursery— *not* in charge of Susan B. Anthony. But we forget, the "Coming Woman" is to give the home and home-life, the kitchen, dining room and nursery a wide berth, and deal with naught but the affairs of State . . . [5]

Old Medical School Building.

5

First Women in Medicine

If there had been prejudice against the admission of women in general, there was especially intense feeling against admitting them to the Medical Department.

Very soon after the Regents had passed their resolution in January of 1870, the Medical Department began to receive applications from women.

At that time there were fewer than half a dozen colleges in the United States where women could get medical training; it would be another half century before the American Medical Association admitted women physicians to membership.

Although women for centuries had undertaken care of the sick and the practice of midwifery, their attempts to enter professional medicine in the nineteenth century met with peculiarly harsh re-

"We certainly did not welcome women students!" one Medical School professor recalled.

Dr. Virginia Watts, '85m, of Ann Arbor, first black woman on campus, and first to receive a medical degree: her career cut short by a tragically early death.

Dr. Amanda Sanford, '71m, first woman to earn a medical degree from Michigan, and with honors: "hooted and showered with abusive notes" at her graduation ceremony.

Women's segregated anatomy class, 1880's. Medical faculty called medical coeducation "an experiment . . . not calculated to increase the modesty of women."

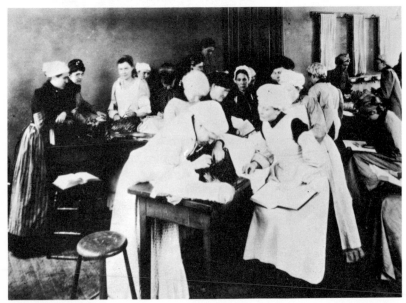

Dr. Alice Hamilton, '93m, became world-renowned authority on industrial medicine, first woman on faculty of Harvard.

Medical clinic, 1890's; Alice Hamilton in front, third from left.

Class in physiological chemistry, 1880's.

buff that probably had its basis in the economic threat. Dr. W. B. Hinsdale, in reply to a question years later about early women students in the Medical Department, remarked, "We certainly did not welcome women students! I think we were afraid they'd take away our patients. But our attitude was not personal."[1]

During Madelon Stockwell's first semester on campus, the medical school faculty was gathering its forces to resist the entry of women students. In March a committee submitted to the Regents a "Memorial on Female Medical Education."[2]

Protesting that they "entertain no prejudice against the medical education of women," they proceeded to present the arguments that had been offered in favor of women studying medicine—that women were mentally qualified, that their sensibilities and sympathies with the sick were more pronounced, that many women would prefer a life devoted to the relief of human suffering rather than the cares of a family, and, finally, "that a proper sense of delicacy demands that the duties of the accoucher (sic) shall be placed in the hands of women."

In rejoinder the gentlemen of the medical faculty wished to point out that

> woman is during a large fraction of each month a quasi-invalid, that her mental and moral manifestations are seriously perturbed at such times . . . that childbearing must incapacitate her during a large part of the period of *utero* gestation . . . and finally, that as child-bearing would be an insuperable obstacle in the way of a female physician, the danger would be that foeticide and infanticide, already alarmingly frequent, would become still more so.

For all these reasons they believed medical coeducation of the sexes was "an experiment of doubtful utility, and one not calculated to increase the dignity of man, nor the modesty of woman."

The only possible solution in their opinion would be to offer instruction to the two sexes in separate classes, which they would be willing to undertake "for a suitable compensation." Even better, suggested the medical professors, let the Regents establish a Female Medical College in Ann Arbor or Detroit.

An undated report of "A Committee of the Medical Department on the Admission of Women," in much the same vein, closes with a pious declaration:

"believing as we do that a State University is designed to be in no sense restrictive except *when the manifest inalienable rights and privileges of one class are abridged or overthrown by establishing those claimed by another.*"[3]

In the summer of 1870 when the Regents met, with literally dozens of applications from qualified women all over the country asking admission to the Medical School, the faculty again sent a plea to the Regents, reaffirming their stand, and declaring that their negative convictions had been confirmed "by the lessons and experience of other schools." They pointed out

the difficulty of restraining improprieties of deportment and checking insubordination in large classes of mixed students assembled in a common lecture room.[4]

But, they added, if they had no choice but to teach women, they would do so—for $500 additional salary apiece.

The Regents voted to admit women to the Medical Department, but to go along with the advice of the medical faculty on separate instruction and pay the professors the extra salary.

Only Regent Willard—who had pushed through the original resolution admitting women to the University—stuck to his guns, stating firmly that "women could properly be admitted to most medical lectures in common with male students."

Amanda Sanford of Auburn, New York, entering in September, 1870, was the first woman to earn a medical degree from the University.

Like Madelon Stockwell she entered with more education and experience behind her than most students, for she had already studied at the Female Medical College in Philadelphia, and had spent a year interning at the New England Hospital for Women and Children in Boston. But she was eager to have the best training possible for her profession, and the Michigan Medical Department was second to none in the country.

Her doctoral thesis, in the archives of the Michigan Historical Collections, was written on "Eclampsia Puerperalis," the dread killer of women in pregnancy and childbirth. Her research was original: she had examined the records of 800 deliveries in the New England Hospital, and she had watched numerous women in the throes of the fatal convulsions that marked the disease. She had read all the available literature in English, German and French, and she knew her subject as well as it could be known in that day; she knew too the tragic and terrible limitations of medical knowledge, for one-half of all women afflicted died. The best treatment, Dr. Sanford wrote, was hot vinegar water on the feet, mustard fomentations on the chest, cupping and drawing blood, chloroform to ease the convulsions, and a cork between the teeth to prevent tongue-biting.

Medical Dean Abram Sager, in his report to the Regents the following year—1871—reported with fairness that the dire predictions of the preceding year about women in medical school had been unfounded, and that "our experiment has been conducted with entire harmony and success."

> We take pleasure in adding that in the front rank of those who have successfully competed for the honors of the Institution will be found the name of a member of the Class of Ladies.[5]

This was Amanda Sanford.

Unhappily, a few days later at the Commencement exercises of the Medical Department, when Amanda Sanford walked to the chancel of the Methodist Church to receive her diploma, with honors, the first woman in the history of the University to be made a Doctor of Medicine, she was hooted and showered with abusive notes from young men students sitting in the balcony.

6

Coeducation and President Angell

The words "coeducation" and "coed" entered the English vocabulary sometime during the 1850's, and it is not impossible that both words originated in Ann Arbor. Though most sources date their appearance in the language as the 1870's, they were certainly used in Ann Arbor as early as the famous State Teachers' Convention of 1855—and probably even earlier.[1]

Both words were disparaging at first. The student *Chronicle* in 1881 called the word "co-ed" a "synonym of ignominy," and in a pamphlet on "The Admission of Women to Higher Education" in 1883 LeComte Stevens calls "co-education"

> an objectionable term, coined scarcely more than a dozen years ago to express certain conditions under which society deemed it improper for young women to have the benefit of higher educational facilities. It will be generally discarded with the decline of prejudice.[2]

If any single person was responsible for removing the stigma from those words, it was James Burrill Angell, third president of the University, who arrived in June of 1871, just a year after women had been admitted.

In holding out all the allurements possible to attract Angell to the job—for the salary of Michigan president, $4500 plus house, was not precisely munificent, and he was already comfortably installed as President of the University of Vermont—Acting President Henry Frieze had reassured Angell that the entering women would not prove troublesome:

The number [of women entering] I am sure would be very inconsiderable and would affect the *character* of the institution but very little anyway; certainly not for the worse. As to *reputation,* which in reality has been the chief ground of objection hitherto (though not confessed) that cannot long be prejudiced.[3]

During his thirty-eight-year tenure President Angell was called upon again and again by educators in the United States and in England to explain and defend his liberal views on women's education. Over and over again—especially in that last third of the nineteenth century, when the experiment was still regarded with anxiety and suspicion—Angell staunchly defended coeducation.

In June of 1872, at the end of his first year, he told the Regents,

If we are still to regard it as an experiment, it must certainly be deemed a most hopeful experiment. The young women have addressed themselves to their work with great zeal and have shown themselves quite capable of meeting the demands of severe studies as successfully as their classmates of the other sex. Moveover, their health seems excellent, they were no oftener absent from sickness than men students.[4]

In 1874 he reported that his general reply to all inquiries on the subject coming to him from outside the University community had been:

The ground once maintained by some, that the women have not the intellectual gifts required to master the severe studies of a collegiate course, seems to be generally abandoned. It would indeed seem difficult to hold it in the face of the brilliant successes of women in our own classes, both in the Literary Department and in the professional schools.[5]

Certainly no president ever did more to afford women within the University equal opportunity with men students—and beyond the University too, when it lay within his power to do so, as it frequently did.

Angell was in all ways an extraordinary man, certainly one of the outstanding educators of the United States. Immensely versatile, of liberal intellectual breadth, he had a clear vision of what he wanted the University to be, and the talent and diplomacy to carry his plans to fruition. His workload was enormous: not only did he handle the administrative details of his office, but he acted as Dean of the Literary Department, as Registrar for all students, he presided at daily chapel (later changed to twice weekly), taught international law and the history of treaties, wrote abundantly, and travelled now and again to deliver important addresses. He handled all his own correspondence, writing hundreds of letters a month in his meticulous legible hand; he had a personal acquaintance with his faculty of 50 men; and it was said that until 1900 he could call by name every one of the 1100 students in the Literary College, and a good many in medicine and law.

Both President Angell and his wife, Sara Caswell Angell, set an example of personal kindness and interest in the women on campus that did much to banish the prejudice they had first encountered. In the Congregational Church on Sundays, Mrs. Angell went out of her way to greet students. When Eliza Mosher, one of the early women medical students—"hen medics," they were called disparagingly on campus and in town alike—was in bed with a sore throat, she wrote home that Mrs. Angell had made and sent over a nice soft custard for her.

And when Alice Freeman Palmer arrived with her father in June of 1872 to apply for admission, an eager pretty seventeen-year-old, but with only scanty preparation in her small town school, she failed her entrance examinations. Later President Angell recalled the incident:

> Her [Academy] teachers regarded her as a child of much promise, precocious, possessed of a bright, alert mind, of great industry, of quick sympathies, and of an instinctive desire to be helpful to others . . . Her preparation for college had been meagre . . . The examiners, on inspecting her work, were inclined to decide that she ought to do more preparatory work. Meantime I had had not a little conversation with her and her father, and had been impressed with her high intelligence. At my request the examiners decided to allow her to enter on a trial of six weeks . . . I need hardly add that it was soon apparent to her instructors that my confidence was fully justified. She speedily gained and constantly held an excellent position as a scholar.[6]

A few years later, at twenty-six, Alice Freeman Palmer was to become president of Wellesley College, the youngest college president in the country.

In addition to judging women as individuals, President Angell was sensitive to an aspect of coeducation that few men in his day were even aware of—that most women had been conditioned from childhood to a sense of intellectual inferiority very difficult to overcome.

In a paper on coeducation he disposed of all the arguments against mixed education, and then added,

> There is a value in the consciousness she has that her education is identical in scope and thoroughness with that of her brother; that circumstance gives her confidence, self-reliance and strength.[7]

The campus that President Angell and the early women students of the 1870's found was simply a bit of open country, where grass grew high and untended in summer and where the unpaved paths were deep in mud or snow the rest of the year. The stark outlines of the nine buildings—for the most part, practical no-nonsense architecture of which the legislators approved—were just beginning to be softened by the fine rows of elms that Cornell President Andrew White had planted and tended during the Civil War, when he taught history at Michigan. Along with delivering his inaugural address at Commencement in June of 1871, President Angell had also laid the cornerstone of University Hall, which would serve for years as home of the Literary College, and with its 60-foot high dome, would be the distinctive mark of the campus profile for decades.

It provided new lecture rooms, chapel, auditorium, and—great stroke of generosity—a "waiting room for the ladies."

On the northeast corner of the campus was the baseball diamond; cricket was still played on the muddy lane of State Street, between the passing buggies and wagons. Not until 1875 would fresh spring water be piped in to campus from a full mile away in the country.

The little academic world of the University had been set up on the old classical pattern of the European universities. It had been President Tappan's particular contribution to bring it closer to the scheme of the Prussian universities, and in the late 1860's the rigorous and demanding German seminar method had been introduced into some departments.

Greek and Latin were still the basis of a liberal education. Class discussion was minimal. There was no question as to whether the courses one studied were relevant to one's life or not. President Angell introduced some interesting changes, giving students far greater freedom of choice in their last two years than most universities did.

Charles Wentworth Dilke, an Englishman on a trip around the world, visited the University and pronounced it:

> probably the most democratic school in the whole world —cheap, large, and practical. There are at Michigan no honor lists, no classes in our sense, no orders of merit, no competition.[8]

This was very nearly completely true. Students were given no grades; they either passed or failed a course, or were "conditioned" —which meant they might try the exam again within a specified period of time.

It cost $10 to enroll in the University, plus $5 a year for "incidentals"—whatever they might be. Students paid approximately $2 a week for room and from $1.50 to $2 for food—plus extra for firewood. Students bargained for their firewood with farmers at the wood-market around the court-house square. There were no dormitories, of course. Rooming houses were mixed more often than not. Men and women shared whatever limited bathing facilities the rooming house provided; plumbing consisted of outdoor privies—a source for the recurrent epidemics of typhoid fever. When the Angells arrived in 1871, they insisted on having a water closet installed inside the President's house; it was the first one in town.

Though there had been such anxiety expressed about the possible danger to their virtue, once women arrived on campus, nobody worried about morals. The University made no special rules for women students; it did not attempt to act *in loco parentis*. Women students had exactly the same privileges as men. Angell wrote in 1881:

> We have never made a single new law or regulation in consequence of their coming . . . The relations of the sexes to each other here are those of well-bred men and women, and are not, in fact, in the least degree embarrassing to us.[9]

The general rule of conduct was that forbidding students from frequenting "gaming or drinking saloons." Nor might they

> be guilty of profaneness or any act of violence—or keep company of persons of ill repute, or be guilty of any other vice; and the use of intoxicating drinks is prohibited. [10]

These rules were, of course, regularly broken by the men students; there were, after all, no fewer than 49 saloons in a town of 7,300.

Even mothers seemed to be more worried about whether their daughters' souls were saved than whether they might be tempted to stray from the path of virtue. And indeed they were right. For these were middle class girls, strictly brought up to the Victorian code of behavior; between the time they spent studying and the time they spent in chapel and church, there was very little time left for extra activities.

Alice Freeman Palmer wrote her family of a typical Sunday in Ann Arbor when she "had her hat off only once between church and bed-time, and that was when I ate my dinner." In between she had been to Bible class, Greek Testament class, a prayer-meeting, and an evening sermon."[11]

The faculty had hoped that the entrance of women would at least provide a refining influence on campus. There is, however, no evidence that things changed materially. Campus life was marked by a good deal of rowdyism and brawling, partly fun, partly serious, much based on traditions of the freshman-sophomore feud.

Fights between groups of freshmen and sophomores might—and did—take place anywhere, in chapel, in corridors, on stairways, even, sometimes, in lecture halls. From time to time the practice of hazing had tragic results, but the faculty appeared helpless to stop the practice.

On Halloween night there were always pranks: the wooden sidewalks might be torn up and sometimes burned, street lamps were smashed, business signs vandalized, and the statue of Ben Franklin standing in the middle of campus painted red or blue.

Just after Madelon Stockwell's admission, in the spring of 1870, members of the sophomore class tore up the sidewalks, and the city fathers, furious, made the whole class pay. In May of 1871 several dozen sophomores and 14 freshmen bolted classes to watch the circus come into town; all were suspended until fall.

Students also had an on-going feud with the local police. There were no mail deliveries; to get their mail students walked to the post-office on the corner of Fourth and Ann, stood in a long line with townspeople. It was a perfect setting for short tempers, especially when a policeman came to be stationed there regularly to break up student fights.

A physics lecture in the late 1880's.

Class Day, Commencement Week, Early 1900's.

7

First Novel about the University

Among the little group of women students in the early '70's was a bright, lively amusing girl named Olive San Louie Anderson— Louie to her family and friends.

Her father, a country doctor in Ohio, had died during her childhood, and Louie Anderson had only with great difficulty won the consent of her widowed mother to attend a coeducational university.

At her Commencement in 1875 Louie Anderson was chosen by the faculty to deliver one of the addresses. Two years later she wrote the first *roman á clef* about life at the University of Michigan, *An American Girl and her Four Years in a Boys' College* (1878).

Long since out of print, the little novel is as patently autobiographical as most youthful first novels. The authenticity of its picture of college life in Ann Arbor in the '70's was vouched for by various classmates of the author. Marginal notes in the copy in the University's Rare Book Room, originally inscribed by a college friend of Louie Anderson's, Cora Agnes Benneson, not only reveal the identity of nearly all the personages mentioned—both faculty and students—but attest to the general veracity of the picture. Only occasionally has Cora Benneson noted "exaggerated" or "no longer true."

Louie Anderson's heroine, Wilhelmine Elliott—Will for short— comes to the University just as the author did, from a small Ohio town, arriving, shy, lonely, and green as grass at the train depot.[1]

"Drive me to the President's house, please," said Will to the hackman, not knowing of any better place to go,·

Student room of Mary Ellen Read, 1889.

Chaucer Hash Club, 1876: "a company of boys and girls club together and get a woman to cook for them." Thrifty and jolly, reported San Louie Anderson.

Coeds arrive at Ann Arbor depot, early 1900's. Early women students came from every part of the country—and from other countries as well.

Scene at Cromell's mixed boarding house, 1902. Rooming houses in the early days were cheerfully coed. Women had no special rules, came and went as they pleased.

Coed room, 1890's.

to find out what she must do first. As they whirled along the avenues of maples, she leaned out of the window with wistful curiosity to see the town that was to be her home for the next four years. The driver stopped before a sombre stone house and handed her out, saying, "This is the place, miss;" then mounted his box and was off. Will tripped up the steps and rang the bell with a beating heart, for she had a wholesome dread of meeting that high dignitary, the President. A broad-faced Irish girl came to the door, and, in answer to the inquiry for the President, said; "La! miss, the President don't live here; there's his house t'other side the campus; this is the hospital, and we have three cases of small-pox."

On foot and in a drizzling rain Will carries her valise to the President's house, where she is told she must go to his office.

The man of affairs sat at his desk, writing, but looked up with a bright smile as Will advanced and offered her letters of introduction.
He shook hands with her and smiled upon her in the most kindly way as he said: "And you came all the way from C——, alone, you tell me, and are not acquainted with any one here, and you want to enter the University? Why, you are a brave girl, I must say!"
"Have any other young ladies applied for admission, and are there very many boys here?"
"I think that you will not be entirely alone, Miss Eliott, for I hear of several young ladies who are intending to be examined for admission; and, as to your last question, I believe there are more than thirteen hundred young gentlemen in all the departments."
"How do you think the girls will be received in college?" asked Will.
"I can tell better some time hence," he replied evasively, "and now I will take you to Mr. Benson, the steward, who will find you a good boarding-place."

Armed with the steward's list Will Elliott makes a discouraging round of rooming houses, whose landladies refuse to take women.

"Mama don't want girls," says the little girl at No. 94 William Street; and "I could not think of taking a lady-student, it's so odd, you know; we can't tell what they might be like," says Mrs. Myers in Thompson Street; and at 59 Jefferson Mrs. Smith sends "a little servant-boy" to inform the heroine: "She hathe not a good opinion of ladieth who wanthe to come to a boyth college."

Discouraged and in tears Will returns to the kindly steward who finds her a place to live with a cousin of his.

She passes the difficult oral and written entrance examinations to enter the Literary Department and appears along with the other girls for the chapel service at the opening of the new semester:

> You see, we have prayers every morning in the law lecture room, as our hall is not done yet; it is an immense room, and the freshmen sit on one side and the sophs on the other, so that the two combustibles are separated by the grave upperclassmen. We girls went fifteen minutes before time, and when we entered the door, we heard the most uproarious din, and on coming up the stairs, found the fresh and sophs joined in mortal combat, while above all rose the chorus, "Saw Freshmen's leg off—*short*!" We were terribly frightened, thinking that someone would surely be killed; but at last we were all in the room and no lives lost . . .

> We poor little wretches did not know where to sit, of course, and not one boy was polite enough or dared to face the crowd and show us a seat; so we kind of edged around into not much of anywhere, but found to our cost that it was in direct line of the missiles between the hostile classes, which missiles consisted of hymn-books, sticks, anything movable; a great apple-core struck me right in the eye, which caused me to see a whole solar system of stars; but I bore it bravely, feeling something of that rapture the old martyrs must have felt—for was I not suffering in the cause of co-education?

Louie Anderson describes another of those freshman-sophomore clashes a bit later:

> We were just coming out of Latin while the sophs were going up to trigonometry, and they met on the stairs and went at it. One sweet-faced boy said, "For Heaven's sake, Phelps, wait until the girls get out of the way!" But that worthy replied, "Damn 'em, they have no business here anyway, and let 'em take their chances!" I was on the last step hurrying to get out of the crowd, when I was pushed violently against the bannisters, making my nose bleed in a most ghastly manner, and, of course, I had no handkerchief, which, you know, is my fortune always in an emergency.

A DANGEROUS EXPERIMENT

She adds a revealing note on the temper of her fellow students in the 1870's:

> I suspect that the faculty have to wink at a great many such things, for this time-honored animosity between those two classes, silly as it is, cannot be stopped at once, and in such an institution the reins have to be held very judiciously, or they would blow the whole faculty up with gunpowder and think nothing of it.

Most of the boys' pranks were of a mild nature, as when the physics room was darkened for an experiment:

> Then some boy makes the sound of a loud kiss, which will pass round the room . . . They do lots of outlandish things, and go to a great deal of trouble to tear up sidewalks and move gates, and one day they managed to get a live donkey upstairs and set him on the platform in the chapel, and when we came to prayers, he stood looking over the Bible as solemn as if he were reading a funeral service . . .

In a delightful chapter the heroine exchanges letters with a friend of hers at Vassar, defending the free-and-easy life of women students at "the boys' university" as opposed to the strict boarding-school atmosphere of the women's college. As to the question her Vassar friend poses—whether girls were really accepted as yet—Will replies:

> You ask if all the boys are reconciled to our being here yet? Most of them, I think, are willing, now that we are really established, to "give the thing a trial." It is very amusing to hear a boy of nineteen or twenty years define woman's sphere, and mark the line which she shall or ought to walk.

On the question of their associations, Will declares:

> Now you wanted to know about the boys—whether they pay us much attention . . . Well, I'll just tell you that you could not carry on many flirtations, and keep up your standing in class too. Some of the girls tried it, but found they must give up one or the other, and with remarkable good sense they chose their books instead of the boys. Yet from the way the wind blows, I should not wonder if one or two matches were made in our class.

Well, what could be more natural and fitting? Where can men and women learn to know each other better than by reciting in the same classes? Why did not your father let you come here with me, instead of sending you off to an old boarding-school, where you don't see a fellow once a month, and are always watched by some old corridor-spy?

The heroine—as her author must have been—was the prototype of the liberated woman of the 1870's. She has already broken loose from her mother's smothering religious orthodoxy, she argues with a clergyman on questions of theology, she wears dresses "short enough to keep out of mud and dust," cuts her long hair off, and of course debates the affirmative on the question, "Shall the ballot be given to woman?"

In 1874—during San Louie Anderson's college days—a referendum amending the Michigan state constitution to permit women to vote was presented to the all-male electorate and resoundingly defeated—135,957 to 40,077.

In her book the young author wrote, "The leaders of the woman-suffrage movement made the university town a basis of operations, and Will was one of the earliest converts." In a stirring debate Will defends her cause and wins over many of her fellow-students.

The question of how they will use their preciously-won educations is also a matter of lively discussion among Will Elliott and her friends.

When her room-mate Clara discusses her future plans of becoming a missionary, Will Elliott declares, "I want to choose some trade or profession for life, as the boys do, and work." She adds, however, "They say that a woman can't have a profession and take care of a family well, and I'd like to show that she can if it is possible."

When she falls in love with a young gentleman bearing the romantic name of Guildford Randolf, her career plans meet with a sharp reverse. Out rowing on the river one evening, Will tells Randolf:

"I think I never told, you, Guildford, that I had fully determined to study medicine before I knew you." "You had!" he exclaimed and looked at her. "Well, I'm glad to be your savior from such a fate."
"I was wondering," she went on, "if you would not think it nice for me to go through the medical department

> while you are in the law; we could be together then, you know."
> A strong expression of disgust came over his handsome face, as he said:
> "Do you suppose that I would ever have a wife who had been familiar with all the disgusting details of a dissecting room? Bah! she would never get rid of it."

At the end of the book the heroine has not yet clearly made her choice. Will Elliott is invited by the faculty—as Louie Anderson was—to be the single girl in her class to speak at Commencement. The topic she chooses is "Women in the Professions."

"Those who expected from the subject," writes the author, "a torrent of invective against the 'gray pre-eminence of man' were disappointed, for it was only a calm, earnest argument for an 'open career for talent.' "

As the book closes, Mr. and Mrs. Lewis, the kind-hearted couple who had accepted women students as roomers when it was a highly unpopular thing to do, are discussing the departure of their seven girl roomers, and especially of Will Elliott:

> "Bless my soul, does that girl think she is going to study medicine?" said Mr. Lewis with an amused laugh. "If she don't marry that pair of handsome eyes that used to be forever coming to study off the same book with her, I'll miss my guess." But his wife retorts: "Oh, you men are so conceited! You think a woman never has an aim in life that she won't leave to go at your beck and call. I have more faith in our Will than that, and we'll see if I'm not right."

As it turned out, neither was right. The author of *An American Girl* went out West after her graduation and taught school to earn enough money for the study of medicine. But in 1886 she drowned in a boating accident on the Sacremento River.

8

Dr. Clarke's Sex-and-Health Bogey

We were haunted in those days by the clanging chains of that gloomy little spectre, Dr. Edward H. Clarke's Sex in Education.[1]

—M. Carey Thomas, President, Bryn Mawr College

Of the three chief arguments that had originally been urged against coeducation on the university level, the first—that women were not intellectually capable of advanced study—had been rather quickly abandoned.

President Angell emphasized in his reports each year that women students at the University were performing as ably academically as men. In fact, he wrote, "There is no branch taught in college which women have not shown themselves entirely competent to master."[2]

The second argument—that women's health would inevitably suffer from the strain of competitive study with men—proved far harder to refute. In 1873 this argument suddenly exploded into national prominence in a little book called *Sex and Education, or a Fair Chance for Girls,* written by a Massachusetts physician, formerly on the medical staff of Harvard College, Dr. Edward H. Clarke. Friends of coeducation suspected that his book had been unofficially inspired by the reluctance of Harvard to open its doors to women.[3]

The title and content of the book were highly provocative in that day, and the book was an overnight best-seller. So great was the demand that seventeen editions were printed in the space of a few years, and it was still being widely quoted in the early years of the twentieth century.

Dr. Clarke's thesis was hardly new. He declared that "the problem of woman's sphere is a problem of physiology pure and simple." A girl could not endure the rigors of coeducation "and retain uninjured health and a future secure from neuralgia, uterine disease, hysteria and other derangements of the nervous system, if she follows the same method that boys are trained in."[4]

Pointing to the rosy-cheeked health of European women as compared to the sickliness of American women—without, of course, citing statistics, for there were none to cite—Dr. Clarke observed:

> Circumstances have repeatedly carried me to Europe, where I am always surprised by the red blood that fills and colors the faces of ladies and peasant girls, reminding one of the canvas of Rubens and Murillo; and am always equally surprised on my return, by crowds of pale, bloodless female faces, that suggest consumption, scrofula, anemia and neuralgia. To a large extent our present system of educating girls is the cause of this pallor and weakness.[5]

The examples he described to contrast the superb health of European and Asian women with Americans might have rendered his viewpoint more than a little suspect:

> I once saw in the streets of Coblentz, a woman and a donkey yoked to the same cart, while a man, with a whip in his hand, drove the team—an exhibition of monstrous muscular and aborted brain development. An American girl, yoked with a dictionary, and laboring with the catamenia, is an exhibition of monstrous brain and aborted ovarian development.[6]

Called once into a Turkish harem to treat one of a dozen wives, Dr. Clarke could not help admiring the harem beauties who crowded around to witness his examination:

> As I looked upon their well-developed forms, their brown skins, rich with the blood and sun of the East, and their unintelligent, sensuous faces, I thought that if it were possible to marry the Oriental care of woman's organization to the Western liberty and culture of her brain, there would be a new birth and loftier type of womanly grace and force.[7]

For his grim picture of American women and the host of mental and bodily ills to which they were prey, Dr. Clarke cited examples out of his own practice. His chief evidence consisted of seven case histories, each more chilling than the last. Curiously enough, although he was attacking coeducation, not a single one of the seven women in his case histories had attended a coeducational college. His avid and anxious readers apparently did not notice the discrepancy.

There was Miss A____, who had attended a female seminary and contracted St. Vitus' Dance from too much study. There was Miss D____ who had entered Vassar at fourteen in excellent physical condition and ended up a case of arrested sexual development:

> The stream of vital and constructive force evolved within her was turned steadily to the brain, and away from the ovaries and their accessories.[8]

And there was the yet sadder case of Miss E____, whose educational dossier Dr. Clarke failed to give, contenting himself with remarking that

> she might have been presented to the public on Commencement Day, by the president of Vassar College or of Antioch College or of Michigan University, as the wished-for result of American liberal female culture . . . Just at this time, however, the catamenial function began to show signs of failure of power . . . Vagaries and foreboding and despondent feelings began to crop out . . . Appropriate treatment faithfully persevered in was unsuccessful in recovering the lost function. I was finally obliged to consign her to an asylum.[9]

Dr. Clarke, of course, knew nothing of hormones or hormonal dysfunction. Nor did he know anything of psychology as we know it today: in 1873 seventeen-year-old Sigmund Freud was just graduating *summa cum laude* from the Sperl Gymnasium in Vienna.

Dr. Clarke was a pamphleteer, and an ardent and persuasive one. His *a priori* arguments were sufficient to prove to thousands of doubtful parents and educators that "identical education of the two sexes is a crime before God and humanity, that physiology protests against and that experience weeps over."[10]

Although the heads of women's colleges and of coeducational universities alike would protest Dr. Clarke's conclusions and insist that the health of their women students was excellent, the author had already forestalled them. He wrote that educators could not possibly judge the heinous effects of coeducation by the *apparent* good health of women students while still in college, for it might be years before the catastrophic results could be discerned, in "grave and even fatal disease of the brain and nervous system . . . in torturing derangements and imperfections of the reproduction system that embitter a lifetime."[11]

In a decade when the coeducational experiment was still very much on trial, Dr. Clarke's final conclusion was a shattering one. He declared flatly that

> if these causes [joint education of the sexes] should continue for the next half-century and increase in the same ratio as they have for the last fifty years, it requires no prophet to foretell that the wives who are to be mothers in our republic must be drawn from trans-atlantic homes. The sons of the New World will have to re-enact, on a magnificent scale, the old story of un-wived Rome and the Sabines.[12]

Coeducation, according to Dr. Clarke, would spell the doom of the race.

In Ann Arbor in 1873 everybody was reading Dr. Clarke's book. The local bookseller reported that he had sold more than 200 copies in a single day, "and that the book bids fair to nip coeducation in the bud."[13]

San Louie Anderson recollected the effect of the book on the university community:

> Dr. Clarke's book was discussed by more than the girls in Clinton Street. The boys read it and delivered their opinion at length among themselves. The president and the faculty read it, and shook their heads doubtfully about the "experiment in coeducation." The ministers . . . took up the question, and particularly the pastor of the Presbyterian Church, Rev. Edmund Allison, felt himself called upon to give his views at length; so, tak-ing Dr. Clarke's book as a basis, he inveighed against the whole woman's movement, both in lectures to his Bible class and in sermons from the pulpit. It was against the canons of the Holy Scriptures that woman should follow the pursuits of men, and that she should wield the saw and scalpel was to the last degree unfit-ting, for, however much she might try to conceal the hateful fact, she was inherently weak, and her persistent efforts to do that for which God never intended her would only result in misery to herself and evil to the race.[14]

The author and heroine of *An American Girl* at once took issue with Dr. Clarke.

> "Sit down, Nell," [says Will] "and read it aloud, for I'd like to know what the dear old humbug has to say against girls." "Why," said Laura with a shocked expression, "Dr. Clarke is one of the most eminent physicians in Boston." "Don't care if he were Aesculapius himself returned from Hades with his shroud on, I would not believe him if he tried to make girls out weak and good for nothing."

After Clara has read the book aloud to the other five girls, the heroine asks,

> "What does the precious doctor propose to do with us after he has cajoled us into believing that we are born and predestined to be invalids from the foundation of the world? Send us home to embroider chair-covers and toilet-sets, I suppose . . .
> Women have washed and baked, scrubbed, cried and prayed themselves into their graves for thousands of years, and no person has written a book advising them not to work too hard; but just as soon as women are beginning to have a show in education, up starts your erudite doctor with his learned nonsense, embellished with scarecrow stories, trying to prove that woman's complicated physical mechanism can't stand any mental strain."[15]

Only on one point did the author of *An American Girl* agree with Dr. Clarke: this was his attack on women's clothing.

As early as 1850 woman's rights activists had begun to denounce the hobbling and irrational fashions of the day, "a dress which imprisons and cripples them." Elizabeth Smith Miller had invented the bloomer costume—publicized by Mrs. Amelia Bloomer—originally a short skirt worn over Turkish trousers. Heads of leading girls' schools and women's colleges had supported dress reform, and many of the early women students at Michigan had adopted the unconventional, looser, shorter "reform" dress.

While Dr. Clarke attributed the major portion of the American woman's ills to the evil effects of coeducation, he did assail as another contributing factor to debility—

> artificial deformities strapped to the spine, or piled on the head . . . Corsets that embrace the waist with a grip that tightens respiration into pain, and skirts that weight the hips with heavier than maternal burdens . . . often

[causing] grievous maladies and [imposing] a needless invalidism.[16]

On the point of clothing the heroine of *An American Girl* was in complete agreement:

> "But, girls, I like what he says against corsets and the abominable way women dress; for I've been of the same opinion since I have been reading about dress reform in *The Woman's Journal*; I am going to burn those new corsets you made me get last week, Clara, and make my dresses shorter; and I'm going to prove to you that the corset, with its concomitant train of evils, has killed more women than ever Noah's flood destroyed."[17]

In a delicious climax to this little scene the emancipated heroine of the 1870's snatches up her corset and throws it into the burning grate.

In the years after 1873 defenders of coeducation called in their own experts and published a refutation of Dr. Clarke's book, calling theirs by the same title, *Sex in Education*. When the Association of Collegiate Alumnae was formed in 1882, one of their first tasks was to study the health of college women.

All the facts and statistics appeared to prove that college women were if anything healthier than non-college women. President Angell reported in 1879:

> The regularity of the life and the deep interest which it awakens and maintains, are manifestly conducive to mental and bodily health.[18]

But Dr. Clarke's book continued to be so successful that in 1880 he published a sequel called *Building a Brain,* adding fresh evidence gleaned from a survey of physicians, members of school committees and school superintendents. They had been asked the simple question: "Is one sex more liable than the other to suffer in health from attendance in school?" Overwhelmingly the men questioned had answered "Female"; only one replied: "Male."[19]

As late as 1905, when the eminent psychologist and President of Clark University, G. Stanley Hall, published his monumental work on the psychology of adolescence, he wrote, ". . . even though he may have 'played his sex symphony' too harshly, E. H. Clarke was right."[20]

9

1896: The Girls get a Dean

In the wake of the anxieties aroused by Dr. Clarke's book, there was a flurry of activity both in women's colleges and in coeducational universities, to counteract any possible evil effects of higher education on women's health. When Smith College opened in 1875, physical education was given status on a level with academic departments, and Smith's first president, Dr. Seelye, took care to refute Dr. Clarke's statements in his inaugural address. Wellesley, opening the same year, offered its students not only physical education but courses in hygiene and physiology.

At the University of Michigan students had been agitating for a gymnasium since the 1860's, but the thrifty Legislature did not believe it was a crucial educational need. In the early 1890's Joshua Waterman of Detroit gave $40,000 for the construction of a gymnasium on condition that an additional $40,000 be raised within a stipulated time.

As plans for fund raising moved ahead among friends and graduates, some skeptical alumnae wondered out loud if the fine prospective gymnasium was to be used by women students too, or if it would be reserved exclusively for men. A committee from the Detroit branch of the Collegiate Alumnae Association called on Waterman to ask the question. He replied, "I have given the money to the women of the University as well as the men."[1]

In spite of Waterman's own statement it soon appeared that if women wanted a gymnasium they would have to find the money themselves. The first efforts of the Detroit alumnae to raise funds for the project were an abysmal failure: people in Detroit did not flock in great numbers to see the dramatic cantata of *The Damnation of Faust* which the ladies had imported from Ann Arbor.

In 1893, however, a group of women—undergraduates and Detroit alumnae—did an absolutely unprecedented thing. They took a train to Lansing to beg the Legislature for a special appropriation to build a gymnasium for women:

> The matter excited a great deal of interest in the Legislature and when the time for the hearing approached the room was crowded with listeners . . . Each member [of the group of women] addressed the Committee on Appropriations of the Legislature. They advanced many cogent arguments, but perhaps the most telling one and the one which influenced the legislators the most was the argument that the women of the University of Michigan were entitled to the appropriation because of the number of women taxpayers in Michigan. All hearers agreed that the University committee had addressed the legislative committee with dignity and with skill.[2]

None of these women could vote, of course, except in local school elections; none could ever vote a legislator in or out of office. When the bill asking for the $20,000 appropriation for a Women's Building came before the Legislature, it lost in a vote of 43 to 42.

Two years later, in early 1895, when the men's gym had meantime been completed and opened, the women students did find a benefactor—in fact, two of them. Regent Levi Lewis Barbour, an 1865 law graduate of Michigan, was to be a champion of women's causes and probably the most important financial benefactor University women ever had. He offered to donate a piece of land in Detroit, valued at $20,000, toward the building of a women's gymnasium. Regent Charles Hebard gave another $10,000. The stipulation was that Michigan women would raise the remaining $15,000 needed.

It was probably Lucinda Hinsdale Stone, now in her eighties, who had persuaded the two Regents to contribute. On her advice the organization of undergraduate women, the League, joined the State Federation of Women's Clubs, of which she was honorary president, so that the help of women all over Michigan could be solicited. Contributions began to come in for the fund, mostly small donations of five or ten dollars, from women in cities and villages all over Michigan.

1896: THE GIRLS GET A DEAN

By the end of the year 1895 plans were drawn up and construction could begin. Although it was built as an annex to the men's gymnasium, it was to be more than a site for physical education. It was to be the focus of women's activities on campus for more than thirty years. The upperclass women of the newly-organized League would issue forth from the Women's Building to the depot to meet the incoming trains of freshmen in the autumn, and help them find their way around campus. In the parlors gentlemen could be entertained, and over the coal stove in the basement kitchen kettles of cocoa could simmer away. There was a splendid auditorium on the second floor, and in a day when Ann Arbor rooming houses provided a bowl and pitcher for washing facilities, the Women's Building boasted not only a dozen gleaming porcelain tubs, but a beautiful little white tiled swimming pool. The whole building, its red brick set with cathedral windows and turrets, its interior lined with varnished golden oak, is a gem of early McKinley baroque.

The Women's Building also housed the offices of the new Dean of Women.

From the time of the admission of women in 1870, Michigan had been one of the few coeducational universities which had devised no special rules for women nor created any special authority to supervise their actions. Angell wrote in 1883:

> We have no rules prescribing their conduct in the hours of recreation, save the general rule that their conduct shall everywhere be such as is becoming.[3]

That men students also took pride in the unusual freedom the University accorded its women students is clear from an editorial in *The Chronicle* in 1873. The author, flaying the restrictive boarding-school atmosphere of most colleges and universities, quotes from the self-report which Northwestern required its women to fill out at regular intervals answering such questions as:

> Have you walked with any gentleman, or accepted company to or from any place or been at any time in the society of gentlemen except at a school exercise without permission?

Denouncing such regulatory measures *The Chronicle* writer declared:

> These boarding schools are doing all in their power to make her dependent in character and uniformly nerveless in her mental action. They piously cut her corset laces and shape her mind as a Chinese lady does her foot. Independent, original womanly women, such as society needs, can no more be developed under such a system than active, energetic manliness in monasteries. Ideas of individual, moral responsibility are not acquired in a condition of mental servitude . . .
> Our fair co-workers in Michigan University . . . are proving in themselves their ability to walk alone, to work alone, to act alone, and all this with womanly modesty and an amount of common sense.[4]

There is no evidence that women students at Michigan had transgressed the bounds of Victorian decorum. But there had certainly been pressures, subtle and not so subtle, on President Angell to establish some kind of supervisory authority over women students, such as both women's and most coeducational colleges had had since their beginnings. Parents had doubtless pressed for it; faculty wives and perhaps Mrs. Angell herself had urged it. However, many years later, in 1922, President-Emeritus Harry Hutchins wrote that it was Regent Barbour's initiative "that led to the establishment of the office of Dean of Women and to the election of the first incumbent."[5]

President Angell thought judiciously that perhaps the ideal solution would be a woman physician to watch over the health of women students, supervise their physical education, and at the same time serve as counsellor-in-residence on their personal problems. He thought he knew the right person for the post, and he now proceeded to lay siege to her.

Eliza Mosher had been one of that first band of pioneer women medical students studying at Michigan in the early '70's. Daughter of a well-to-do Quaker farming family in New York state, Eliza had set her heart on studying medicine when tuberculosis—that dread nineteenth-century killer—had taken the lives of two beloved brothers and a niece in her big, sprawling devoted family. She felt she must find out what caused the disease. Amanda Sanford—who was to be the first woman graduate of Michigan's Medical Department—was a school friend of Eliza Mosher's at the Friends' Academy in Union Springs, New York; together the girls had sent for catalogs from the recently-opened Female Medical College of Philadelphia.

1890's: The Girls Got a Dean and Plenty of Exercise.

Dr. Eliza Mosher, '75m, first Dean of Women and first woman professor at the University: "Death on corsets, tyrant on exercise . . . designed a bicycle seat kind to girls' anatomies."

With the new Barbour Gymnasium, 1896, physical education became a requirement.

Girls' Field Day and Lantern Night, 1911.

Women students on a sleighing party, 1920's.

Freshman Week, 1931: Dean Alice Lloyd, Dr. Margaret Bell, Miss Ethel McCormack.

But Eliza's widowed mother, despite her Quaker beliefs in woman's equality, was scandalized at the thought of her daughter entering such an all-male profession:

> "I would sooner pay to have thee shut up in a lunatic asylum, Eliza," she had said, "than to have thee study medicine."[6]

While Amanda Sanford went off to Philadelphia to study medicine, Eliza stayed home on the farm, attending public lectures on anatomy and physiology, buying medical books to study by lamplight on winter evenings, practicing dissection on the variety of animals available to a farm woman.

In the end she won her mother's consent to work for a year as "amateur interne" at the New England Hospital for Women and Children in Boston: "I have made up my mind," said her mother, "that thee is in earnest." And her mother chaperoned her as far as Boston.

Eliza herself described the apprenticeship as a kind of nursing traineeship, but she learned almost at once to deliver babies, delivered twelve that winter without assistance, and in her lifetime would deliver hundreds. To her everlasting pride she never lost one.

Eliza remembered long after the day in April of 1870 when news reached the all-female staff of the New England Hospital that Michigan University had opened its doors to women medical students. The five young women working in the lab "abandoning their seemly demeanor . . . joined hands and danced about the laboratory table." All five applied at once to Michigan; Emma Call and Amanda Sanford enrolled the following autumn, Eliza Mosher a year later.

Eliza Mosher had been an excellent student. One day Dr. Alonzo Palmer asked her to prepare a cancer specimen as a demonstration to the segregated women's anatomy class. She did it so well that he proposed she repeat her demonstration before the much larger men's class. Eliza recalled afterward the terror she felt as she stood in the pit of the amphitheatre and looked up at the sea of male faces staring down at her. When she had finished, however, the entire class applauded her.[7]

After her graduation from Michigan in 1875 Dr. Mosher had practiced in Poughkeepsie, had served as resident physician to Vassar College students, and had been prison physician at the

Massachusetts Reformatory for Women. She was engaged in a thriving private practice in Brooklyn, New York, when President Angell's letter arrived, inviting her to Ann Arbor:

> My dear Dr. Mosher [he wrote on August 1, 1895] Are you not getting tired enough of the whirl of a great city to begin to long for the charms of a small one?

The Angells had made a special point of befriending the early women medical students, in a day when they were often shunned even by students in the Literary Department. President Angell knew Eliza Mosher well; he thought her talent and experience would fit her perfectly for the new office he envisioned. He described the new gymnasium for women and offered her the post of "Vice-Dean", defining the duties very broadly:

> My present idea is that her relations [with women students] should be personal and advisory rather than formally official and authoritative.

He wanted her to be "a guide, philosopher and friend" to women students.[8]

Eliza Mosher's reply was cautiously receptive, but she wished her appointment to be as professor of gynecology in the Medical Department.

To this Dean Victor Vaughan could not—or would not—agree. There was, he explained, no chair vacant in the Medical Department. At least one woman—Dr. Lena C. Leland—had held since 1881 a minor appointment in the Medical Department, as Assistant Demonstrator in Anatomy, but no woman had ever had faculty status. Dr. Vaughan proposed instead to Eliza Mosher that she assist him by instructing the women of the Literary Department in hygiene:

> There are many questions in hygiene, especially those concerning sex, which I cannot very well and do not discuss.

But Eliza Mosher had her own professional pride; it seemed to her only right that her appointment be within the Medical Department of the University, since she was a physician. She declined Angell's offer.

Her life was a very full one, and she was not by any means certain she wanted to change it. Besides her busy Brooklyn practice, treating chiefly women and children, Eliza Mosher had always applied her lively, versatile mind to a host of peripheral problems. She was intensely interested in questions of public health, of sanitation, and especially of preventive medicine. She had designed a kindergarten chair and other school furniture that would encourage good posture, and a new seat for the New York street railways that would do the same thing. Remembering with sorrow a young niece who had literally tortured herself to death by wearing a tightly-laced corset night and day to produce the desirable wasp waist, Dr. Mosher now designed a loose-fitting underwaist for women to supplant the unhealthy corset. When Dr. Angell's first letter came, she was designing a bicycle seat for girls, which, she hoped, would be kinder to their anatomies and thereby encourage more women to healthful exercise. She would always be a tyrant on the question of exercise.

How President Angell handled Eliza Mosher's refusal was characteristic of his consummate diplomatic talent. He accepted her refusal graciously and regretfully. Then he mailed her the architect's plans for the new women's gymnasium, asking her advice on certain questionable points. A gymnasium specifically for women was still a novel idea in the 1890's. Dr. Mosher plunged into those plans with her usual enthusiasm, returning them to Angell with a list of useful suggestions. She also outlined a proposal for a new four-year course in physiology and hygiene, which was to include instruction in psychology and public health—both very innovative ideas in that day.

Angell reopened negotiations. He offered her a post as Dean of Women, with supervision over the health of women students, and all the activities of the women's gymnasium. She would hold a lectureship in hygiene in the Literary College, carrying the title and salary of full professor. Eliza Mosher acquiesced. She arrived in Ann Arbor with her complete household, including a favorite horse, a handsome carriage and two live-in maids, to take up her new duties in the autumn of 1896 just as the Women's Building was opening.

Although Eliza Mosher's six-year reign as Dean of Women and lecturer in hygiene was memorable to women students on the campus, it was not from their point of view an unqualified success.

A DANGEROUS EXPERIMENT

To her friend, Alice Freeman Palmer, Eliza Mosher had written, asking what in the world a dean of women *did*. Mrs. Palmer, who had filled the post for a time at the University of Chicago, replied somewhat evasively:

> [The girls] will see that you are appointed not because you are a woman, and "to keep an eye on them,"—the only suspicion you will have to combat!—but because you are the best possible person to be found to do a great piece of work for the University and for its women especially . . . Dear Dr. Angell needs you, and you will add much comfort to all who are working for the *best things.*

Her appointment was duly reported in the New York papers, and *The New York Tribune* commented:

> The students in Michigan University, both men and women, are not dominated. They are supposed to be old enough to take care of themselves and are thrown on their own responsibility. There are no dormitories with matrons in charge . . . Dr. Mosher will exercise general intellectual and moral oversight over them.

Eliza Mosher entered on her new duties with all her usual energy and enthusiasm—and probably more than a trace of the hearty authority she had brought to her post in the Massachusetts Women's Reformatory. Nearly six feet tall, of stalwart frame, with steel-rimmed spectacles and a crown of white hair worn in pompadour style, Eliza Mosher was an intimidating figure.

She instituted health examinations for entering students, marched them up and down, measured them from head to toe, criticized their posture and denounced their corsets. She hired instructors in calisthenics and made physical education a required course. She herself designed the gymnasium uniform: it consisted of knee-length bloomers made of no less than twelve yards of black serge, worn over a white flannel under-blouse.

She believed in sensible, no-nonsense clothes for college. When a freshman girl's mother asked for advice on suitable clothing for the Ann Arbor climate, Dr. Mosher advised "long, fleece-lined underwear, heavy warm woollen dresses, sensible low-heeled shoes."

One student, Ellen Bach, recalled:

> She marched us around like a regiment of soldiers. It
> was useless to say one word against physical education.
> Dr. Mosher called anyone who didn't like it "just plain
> lazy."

She vaccinated three hundred girls during her first year, and
because it was still a somewhat primitive procedure she had to fill
a classroom with cots for girls ill from unfavorable reactions. It was
undoubtedly a very sensible procedure, for Dr. Mosher remembered vividly a smallpox epidemic at the University in the 1870's when
30 medical students became infected from an autopsy and at least
one had died.

Eliza Mosher took very seriously her "moral oversight." Rules
for social conduct were drawn up and she saw that they were
strictly observed. Girls travelling to and from college were required
to travel by day if they were going by coach and by pullman sleeper
if at night. Once a freshman girl going home for vacation sat up all
night in a coach and found herself promptly suspended. Even when
her mother wrote President Angell protesting that his Dean of
Women harbored evil thoughts, President Angell upheld the Dean,
and the girl transferred to another college.

For her hygiene lectures Dr. Mosher had devised a unique set of
visual aides to demonstrate the female anatomy. She had sewed
out of colored silk and ribbons a whole set of bright-hued internal
organs—heart, liver, uterus, ovaries, with yellow ribbon intestines
and red and blue arteries and veins. These she would drape over
herself during the lectures. A student later recalled:

> Her lectures on anatomy and physiology were horrible
> to us. She'd try on her silk organs like a dress and talk
> about them freely. It made us shudder.

Undoubtedly Dr. Mosher's straight-forward lectures on anatomy
and hygiene as well as questions of public health, were beneficial
to women students in a day when there was little discussion of sex
and the physical anatomy.

It was doubtless a source of deep disappointment to Eliza
Mosher that so few of the girls came to her for advice and counsel
on their personal problems. She was apparently more popular with
the male students, often had one or two living under her roof
rent-free. She knew how to talk to the young men, enjoyed their
company, invited them in for her excellent Friday night dinners.

Partly for reasons of health—partly also because she was not really happy in the job—Eliza Mosher resigned in 1902 and eventually returned to her private practice.

The new Dean, Mrs. Myra Beach Jordan, '93, was not a physician, and she viewed her job in a somewhat different way. Mainly she set up a system of rooming houses for women students which were inspected, supervised and approved by her office—the League houses that preceded dormitories. The office of Dean of Women segregated housing, and the special rules and regulations designed to guard the morals of women students would continue into the 1960's.

10

How the First Graduates Used
Their Education

*We have already said that the coeducational rights of women
are simply those of all human beings—What we claim is that
no one knows as yet what women are, or what they can do—*[1]
—Caroline Dall, 1861

"Of what use are degrees to be to girls," President Woolsey of
Yale had wondered in 1858, "unless they addict themselves to
professional life"—an idea, he was certain, that would be met with
ridicule. To President Walker of Harvard the question of admitting
women to universities depended on whether "we"—we men, that
is—"propose to educate females for public or private life."[2]

As for the females themselves, they had not, as we know, been
consulted.

But when the decision was finally theirs, thirteen and more years
later, when they had finally gone through the glorious ritual of
Commencement Week, had negotiated the nine steps up and down
from the platform in their trailing skirts and high-buttoned shoes
to clutch the first precious diplomas inscribed with girls'
names, what in the end did they do with their degrees? What did
they do with their lives and those hard-won educations?

Annie Peck, who graduated in the famous class of '78—a class
noted for its unusual proportion of brilliant men and women—may
not have been typical in her choice of life; but she was surely typical
in the way she sensed its epic possibilities.

On the placard that advertised her lecture tours ("Queen of the

Climbers," it reads, "Lectures with Stereopticon"), Annie stands against her mountain back-drop, climber's stick in hand, climber's rope dangling from her waist, on her head at a rakish angle a hat not unlike the ones that went up San Juan Hill. The Singer people gave away a whole packet of Annie Peck pictures with every sewing machine, so that ladies pumping away at the treadle could sigh with admiration at one of their sex who had launched into the world's most daring occupation.

After her graduation Annie Peck had taught Latin at Purdue University, then spent a year in Athens as the first woman student at the American School of Classical Studies, returned home to lecture for several years in Greek and Roman archeology at Smith College.

At 40 Annie had had enough of school teaching; she wanted to climb mountains. She tried the Alps first, was one of only three women in the nineteenth century to climb the Matterhorn, and the only woman to negotiate the nearly vertical Funffinger Spitze, most perilous rock climb in Europe.

From the Alps she went on to the Central and South American peaks, unconquered still in the early years of this century. She began with Mount Orizaba and Popocatepetl. At 54, writing her own press release, she announced to the world that she was about to tackle Mount Sorata in Bolivia:

> It will be the loftiest height yet reached on the surface
> of the earth, breaking the world's record in mountain
> climbing. Those who know me feel certain of my success,
> as I have never yet failed in anything I have undertaken.
> I will succeed or I will never come back.[3]

She did reach the summit of Sorata, with the President of the University of New Mexico and two Swiss guides. At 58 she went on to Peru; it took three attempts and four years to scale the peak of Mount Huascaran, then believed to be the highest mountain in the western hemisphere. The Peruvians were so impressed at the wiry, indomitable, gray-haired American lady—who, said the Peruvian ambassador in Washington, knew more about his country than he did—that they named a mountain for her: *Cumbre Annie Peck,* to this day.

In between expeditions she lectured and wrote; a copy of one of her books on South America was reported to be seen on Teddy

Roosevelt's desk in the White House. "Miss Peck in all her mountain climbing discards skirts," one journalist reported. "She wears knickerbockers or loose bloomers." But when Annie Peck appeared on the lecture platform, it was in sweeping creations of white silk and lace, as handsome and patrician as a Sargent portrait, with jewels in her ears, and a flower in her beautifully coiffed hair.

In 1919 she became a flying enthusiast, covered South America by plane. She was 84 when she died in 1935: until a year or so before her death she kept in trim by climbing a modest mountain or two in New Hampshire.[4]

Though Annie Peck was the only alumna to win world-wide renown in her particular field, numbers of Michigan women who earned diplomas before 1900 went on to make their mark in fields of medicine, of scholarship, of education, of social service.

The end of the nineteenth century and the opening of the twentieth appeared to hold enormous promise for women. Their right to higher education had been won. The concept of coeducation, especially in publicly-supported universities, appeared to be firmly established. Although women had not yet won the vote, and although restrictive laws still inhibited control over large areas of their lives, most educated women felt that it was only a question of time before they would win autonomy and acceptance in every area of society.

They had a definite character, those Michigan women graduates of the '70's and '80's, independent, determined, a bit audacious, and with it all, those lofty Victorian "moral ideals." For the four years of college they lived, a tiny minority in the all-male world of the campus, joined by the bond of their very special circumstances, highly selected to begin with, exceptionally ambitious, dedicated students. They *had* to prove themselves, *had* to make good on the world's terms. All their lives most of the early Michigan alumnae kept their sense of group pride and community, returned joyfully to class reunions, felt strong loyalty to the alma mater that had only grudgingly agreed to nourish daughters as well as sons.

President Angell described very sensitively the sororital bonds of the early women classmates:

> The girls were studied by others and themselves a little unduly. Heartily welcomed everywhere though they were, they could not take what each day brought as a matter of course. Being pioneers and representatives of

many who would come afterwards, they were burdened with a sense of responsibility. According as they conducted themselves, their sisters would have ampler or narrower opportunities. Such conscious conditions insure uprightness, but are hardly so favorable for ease and the graces. They had at least the good effect of banding the girls together and uniting the little group by something like a family tie.[5]

In 1875 the founder of Wellesley College, Henry F. Durant, beseeched President Angell's help in filling the first professorships of his brand-new college. Angell sent him one of his best history graduates, Mary Sheldon Barnes; in the following years he dispatched more of his top women scholars, until he could point with pride to the fact that six Michigan women were serving on the Wellesley College faculty. They included Angie Chapin, A.B. '75, Professor of Greek; Eva Chandler, A.B., '78, Professor of Mathematics; Katharine Coman, A.B., '80, Professor of History.

But by far the most distinguished he sent to Wellesley—indeed, the outstanding woman graduate of Michigan before 1900—was Alice Freeman Palmer, who went from Professor to Chairman of the History Department at Wellesley, and at 26 became President, the youngest and certainly the prettiest college president in the country. She was one of those persons whose impact on their contemporaries is only partly explained by the arithmetical sum of their accomplishments, but owes far more to the grace and charm of an exceptional personality.

President Angell, for one, was thoroughly captivated; and Alice was often invited as a student to the President's house. She was, Angell said later,

> the radiant center of a considerable group whose tastes were congenial with her own. Without assuming or striving for leadership, she could not but be to a certain degree a leader among these . . . Her nature was so large and generous, so free from envy, that she was esteemed by all her comrades, whether they cherished exactly her ideals or not. Wherever she went, her genial outgoing spirit seemed to carry with her an atmosphere of cheerfulness and joy. No girl of her time in withdrawing from college would have been more missed than she.[6]

Though she had initially failed her entrance examinations, Angell had recognized her intellectual potential. He recalled later talking with a mother whose son was in the University with Alice, and who used to come home saying, "There's a girl in my class who knows everything—everything!"

Unlike some of her classmates, Alice Freeman was feminine rather than feminist. Harriet Holman Bishop remembered:

> "Eleven of the classmates who graduated together in 1876 were women; sixty were men. The women formed a close group who made lifelong friendships, but Alice Freeman counted many of the men her friends too."[7]

And though most of the women in the Literary Department shunned acquaintance with the women of the Medical Department, Alice made lasting friendships with the "hen medics," such as Eliza Mosher, as well. "Oh Alice!" Harriet Bishop went on. "Alice knew everybody, even the janitors. She never had a thought for what people would say."[8]

No American girl had ever earned a Doctor of Philosophy degree. In 1874 there were only four women Ph.D's in the whole world. When Alice Freeman first taught school after graduation, she planned to return to Michigan and work on a Ph.D.; she saw no reason why she should not be the first American woman to win the highest degree. Five years out of college, she became President of Wellesley; a year later, in 1882, Michigan conferred on her an honorary Doctor of Philosophy degree—the first the University ever granted to a woman.

As the Graduate Department of the University developed in the last quarter of the nineteenth century, women began to earn an increasing proportion of the advanced degrees. By 1900 eleven women had earned Ph.D. degrees on examination; the first had been June Rose Colby, A.B. '75, A.M., '82, later Professor of English at Illinois State Normal School, who received her Ph.D. in 1886.

Graduate students of both sexes were still sufficiently rare to be noticeable among the student body, who called them "posts" or "P.G.'s." Lucy Maynard Salmon, A.B. '76, left her $700-a-year teaching job in an Iowa high school to return to Michigan in 1882 and work for a Master's degree in history. "President Angell calls me "the patriarch," she wrote a friend, "and asks me if I do not feel like a relic of past ages. It did seem a little strange at first to have no acquaintance among the students, and I didn't know but I might be mistaken for an intellectual and geological specimen . . . "[9]

Lucy Salmon's Master's thesis on the appointing powers of the American President was published by the American Historical Association, and brought her national renown, both in circles of scholarship and of government. One federal official addressed a letter of compliment to Lucy M. Salmon, Esquire, and when she gently set him right as to her sex, he replied:

> It did not occur to me that a woman was the author of a work so logical in style and upon a subject so much out of the range of studies generally selected by women.[10]

Besides Wellesley College, other women's colleges drew heavily on Michigan graduates for their staffs. Lucy Salmon became Professor, then Chairman of the History Department at Vassar College.

Another early alumna, Mary A. Byrd, A.B. '78, served for years as Professor of Astronomy and Director of the Observatory at Smith College. At Michigan she had been considered one of the most brilliant students of her class, but more than a little eccentric, and totally independent, paying as little attention to matters of dress as the heroine of San Louie Anderson's novel. In 1906 Mary Byrd resigned after 19 years on the Smith faculty, in protest against the college's acceptance of "tainted money" from John D. Rockefeller and Andrew Carnegie.

It was, of course, far more difficult for women to secure teaching posts at coeducational colleges than at women's colleges. It was totally impossible for a woman to teach in a men's college.

First woman to hold a teaching post at Michigan, Louisa Reed Stowell, B.S. '76, M.S. '77, had married her professor, Dr. Charles Henry Stowell. There were no rules of nepotism in that day, and Louisa Stowell served for years as Assistant in Microscopic Botany, while her husband was Professor of Histology. Of several women teaching assistants on the Michigan faculty in 1899, only two—Alice Hunt in drawing, and Fanny Langdon in zoology—held a rank as high as instructor. Fanny Langdon was already well-launched on a career of scientific research, with several notable publications to her credit, when she died prematurely in 1899.

First woman on the faculty at Leland Stanford University was also a Michigan graduate, the same Mary Sheldon Barnes, '74, whom President Angell had first sent to Wellesley. Mary Barnes had left Wellesley to study at the newly-founded Newnham College of Cambridge University. Later Mary Barnes and her husband, Earl Barnes, both taught at Stanford, another of the very first husband-wife pairs in the American academic world.

Next to teaching, the profession that drew the largest number of women graduates through the turn of the century was medicine.

In the years before 1900 women had made up an increasing proportion of the medical classes at Michigan. In 1880 19.3 per cent of the graduating class were women; in 1890, more than 25 per cent; and in 1900, 24 per cent became doctors of medicine.

Of the nearly 500 women physicians graduated through 1900, a number had chosen to become medical missionaries. Dr. Leonora Annette Howard-King, Dr. Mary Stone and Dr. Ida Kahn worked as missionaries in China. It was a view of the work of these women that so impressed former Regent Levi Lewis Barbour on a trip around the world, that he founded the Barbour Scholarships for Oriental women.

The first two black women to graduate from Michigan, Mary Lucy Harding and Virginia Jane Watts, both chose to put their brains and skills to work to help their own people.

Virginia Watts, daughter of an Ann Arbor family, enrolled for two years in the Literary Department of the University (1878 to 1880), then entered medicine and earned her degree in 1885. She practiced medicine in East Saginaw, then in the Tuberculosis Sanitarium at Dansville, New York. Whether she had gone to Dansville already ill of tuberculosis, or whether she contracted the disease there is not clear, but she died at her family's home in Ann Arbor in 1891.

Mary Lucy Harding, of Detroit, enrolled at the University with advanced standing in August of 1880, and earned her Bachelor of Philosophy degree in the Latin Scientific Department in 1882. Soon after her graduation she went to Africa to work as a missionary under the Presbyterian Board of Foreign Missions, remaining there until 1889. When she returned in 1889, she taught school for a time in Little Rock, Arkansas, and in the Presbyterian Academy in Pine Bluff. Soon afterward, all trace of this intriguing young woman was lost; inquiries sent by the Alumni Records Office were returned, marked: "No information as to whereabouts."

Besides teaching, medicine, and missionary work, two occupations that served human needs very directly were becoming professionalized in the 1880's and 1890's, and offered new choices to college women: social work and nursing.

A newly-aroused interest in social welfare, and the founding of the settlement houses in the big cities, brought a demand for trained social workers, and colleges began to add new courses to their curricula.

Like the practice of medicine, nursing had been one of the oldest professions in which women actively engaged. Three centuries before Florence Nightingale and Clara Barton began to organize nursing services during the Crimean and Civil Wars, Elizabeth Alkin, an energetic and imaginative woman printer in England, had set up the first nursing service in the British Navy. Not until the late nineteenth century did the training of nurses become part of a system of higher education. In 1891 the Regents authorized the Medical Department to establish a training school for nurses within University Hospital. Within a few years the School of Nursing had set up the first four-year curriculum in nursing education in the country and had increased its enrollment from eight to twenty students by 1900.

While the numbers of women entering medicine had climbed steadily until 1900, the number of women entering law remained very small. By 1900 only 41 women had earned law degrees at Michigan; it continued to be one of the most difficult fields for women to enter, and one most highly discriminatory against women.

Law Professor Bradley M. Thompson, interviewed by a *U. of M. Daily* reporter in 1899, thought that women with law degrees might "go into newspaper work or into insurance—and all kinds of office work." He added:

> "I do not think the women are well adapted to court practice. It is too much like a football game . . . Besides the women marry pretty soon and that is the end of their law practice."[11]

Some women law graduates married lawyers—and probably continued to practice in partnership. Others remained single, and carried on active practices.

Among the latter was Cora Agnes Benneson, A.B. '78, LL.B. '80, who had been refused entrance in Harvard Law School and had been one of two women students in her law class at Michigan. After collecting still another Michigan degree—Master of Arts—Miss Benneson travelled around the world, making a study of the judicial systems of various countries. In 1894 she was admitted to the Massachussetts bar and began an active law practice in Cambridge; according to press notices, she was never defeated in a court case. An ardent supporter of woman suffrage, Miss Benneson took issue with her Michigan law professors on the subject of women in law, declaring that success in law was not a matter of sex, and that women were especially well adapted to probate work and trusteeships.

Another Michigan law graduate, Octavia Bates, A.B. '77, LL.B. '96, daughter of a wealthy Detroit family, told a *U. of M. Daily* interviewer in 1899 that she had studied law "for the purpose of fitting herself to deal more fundamentally with social questions." Active in women's causes, Miss Bates was the only American delegate to speak at the International Council of Women meeting in London in 1899. Her address on "Women and the Law" created something of a sensation and was reprinted in nearly every city in Europe and America. Her speech was brought to the attention of Queen Victoria, who summoned her to the palace for tea and to question her further. The Queen, said the London press, "was deeply impressed with the spirit of progressiveness of American women."

Like most of her generation, Octavia Bates remained deeply loyal to the University—and she proved it in one of the nicest, most practical ways. When she died in 1911, she left $20,000 to the law library, and named the University residuary legatee of her sizable estate, that remainder to be used to enlarge the library of the Literary Department.

It appeared, after all, quite as President Woolsey of Yale had feared, that Michigan women graduates might become addicted to professional life. Some even audaciously combined their professions with marriage—but this was a rare feat indeed in that day.

Of the women who graduated from Michigan before 1900, only a little over half married. Madelon Stockwell married a classmate, Charles Turner, in April of 1873, just after he received his law degree. The young pair—the very first of uncounted Michigan couples who would marry in the hundred years after—went to a favorite professor, the Reverend Benjamin Cocker, to ask for his official blessing. He gave them his blessing, but added that he was excusing his class the next day so that he could go to Kalamazoo to lecture on the evil effects of coeducation.

President Angell declared optimistically that he thought coeducational marriages had the best possible chances of success:

> Many of the happiest marriages I have known resulted from coeducation. Are we not justified in maintaining that an acquaintance of four years in the class-room furnishes as good ground for a wise choice of husband or wife as a chance acquaintance in a ballroom?[12]

And Alice Freeman Palmer agreed, believing that "coeducational marriages seldom appear in the divorce courts."[13]

Her husband wrote of her:

> I think her own manners—as quiet and free among men as among women—owed much of their naturalness to the fact that at no period of her life did men become strange.[14]

Certainly the anxieties of early opponents of coeducation—that the University would be turned into a "courting academy"—proved groundless. The percentage of Michigan women graduates before 1900 who married—about 51.5 per cent—was only slightly more than the proportion of graduates of women's colleges who married, and substantially less than the 72.5 per cent of married females in the general population.

Some of the reasons for the high proportion remaining single are clear. For one thing, unlike the young men entering college fresh out of high school at an average age of 19, many of the women students of the '70's and '80's were several years older, had taught school or studied elsewhere, before they collected either the money or the self-confidence needed to attempt admission at a great university. Annie Peck was 24, Octavia Bates 27, Mary Byrd 27, Sarah Dix Hamlin 26, when they came to Michigan. They were highly motivated, serious students, investing themselves in professional preparation.

Even for the younger women, a sense of pride in their own achievement, of participation in that early sisterhood of professionals, sometimes made the choice between marriage and a career a painful one. It was the first time in history that middle class women were asked to make that choice. In earlier centuries women had not faced such a dilemma—not because they did not work outside their own households, for very many did take an active part throughout their adult lives in all kinds of crafts and trades, as the women printers had. But as industry had moved away from the home, it had become less and less acceptable for middle class women to leave home to work; the image of a working wife appeared eventually to be a kind of slur on a middle class husband's masculine pride.

When Alice Freeman, as President of Wellesley, fell in love with Harvard Professor George Herbert Palmer, her decision of marriage versus career was, says a recent biographer, "excruciatingly difficult"—far more difficult than her husband implied in his account.[15] It was an either-or decision, for although the Wellesley trustees offered any number of alternatives to Palmer, including the presidency of Wellesley either alone or jointly with his wife, he declined all offers and persuaded Alice to resign the presidency "for reasons of health." Women throughout the country wrote her, "denouncing her as vacillating, stubborn or disloyal," though others also wrote sympathetically of her dilemma.

When Dr. Amanda Sanford, first woman to graduate from the University's Medical Department, married Patrick Hickey of Auburn, New York, in 1884, her friends expressed shock and disappointment in her, partly from sectarian prejudice—a Quaker marrying an Irish Catholic!—partly out of fear that Amanda would give up her profession. But Dr. Sanford-Hickey simply added to her practice of medicine the new job of mothering her husband's brood of children from a previous marriage. She was in large part responsible for raising money for the first hospital in Auburn; only her untimely death from pneumonia in 1894 put an end to a happy active life.[16]

Obviously many men did not care to marry one of the college-educated, emancipated women they met in their classes. As one writer, Henry T. Finck, wrote in 1901:

> Men's right to decide what women should be like is "inalienable and eternal." Men will continue to make women what they want them to be by marrying those who correspond to their ideals.[17]

But as James Rowland Angell wrote in 1904, many women pre-
ferred self-support to marriage on the terms they found marriage
offered to them.[18]

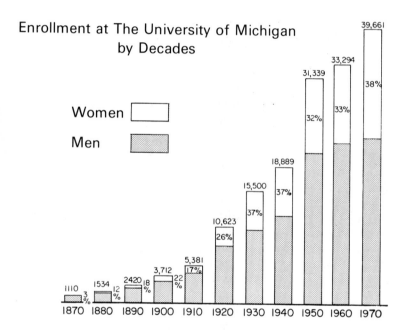

Enrollment at The University of Michigan
by Decades

11

Of Clubs and Women Professors

*Women do their best work when they are allowed to do it,
not as women, but as human beings.*
—Margery Fry, Principal of Somerville College, Oxford

In June of 1890 the University conferred an honorary Doctor of
Philosophy degree on Lucinda Hinsdale Stone for her remarkable
contributions to the education of women.

The woman who had never attended college herself had not only
been instrumental in opening the University's doors to women but
had encouraged hundreds to continue their higher learning, and
had played a leadership role in Michigan's club movement, the
nineteenth century's answer to continuing education for women.

Only a hundred years ago the lives of most middle class married
women, especially in the rural areas of America, were narrowly cir-
cumscribed by the taxing chores of a still unmechanized household
and by the twenty to thirty years spent in rearing large families.
For most women the church was their single social outlet. The
hundreds of women's clubs that sprang up in the latter half of the
nineteenth century were a link between the home and a larger
world outside; they drew into their membership thousands of
women, middle-aged, middle class, of conservative mind, giving
them an outlet for their frustrated energies, an interest in matters
of public concern and a means to self-education.

As early as 1852 Lucinda Stone had founded the first such club
in Michigan, the Ladies' Library Association of Kalamazoo, which
had not only created a public library for the town, but had kept it

stocked with books and staffed with volunteers. A few years later, after attending meetings of the New England Woman's Club in Boston, Lucinda Stone returned to Kalamazoo and reorganized the Library Association into a woman's club with classes in history, art, literature, current events.

The club was widely imitated, and Mrs. Stone herself visited dozens of little groups of women all over Michigan and adjoining states, encouraging them and helping them to form their own organizations—library clubs, clubs for civic improvement, clubs for general self-culture.

In 1890 the largest New York women's club, Sorosis—formed in 1868 when the New York Press Club refused to admit women to its dinner for Charles Dickens—invited other groups to join in the General Federation of Women's Clubs. Lucinda Stone, one of the promoters, was named honorary vice-president, along with Julia Ward Howe and Jennie June Croly. By 1900 the G.F.W.C. counted 150,000 members, supported the Progressive movement in public affairs and social reform, began to lobby for regulatory legislation benefiting women and children. And the immense group now added its weight to the thrust for women's suffrage. For the first time in history a large group of middle-class women were organized as an effective pressure group.

Lucinda Stone called the club movement "post-graduate education for women, which more than Vassar and Smith and Wellesley Colleges are the real instituions at present educating American women."[1] Like others of that first generation of emancipated women, she was inclined to view in rosy terms a future where women would change the world:

> These clubs are established in almost every little village in our state—in many a country neighborhood, and they are preparing as we venture to prophesy, for generations close upon our own, such a civilization as the world has never seen before, truly a new renaissance of which it may be said, *dux femina facti.*

It had been in large part for her activity in the club movement that Lucinda Stone received her honorary degree in 1890—only the second woman in the history of the University to be made an honorary Doctor of Philosophy.

The degree-conferring at that time was not a ceremonial occasion. Lucinda Stone was simply notified by telegram that the award had been granted her. It was unfortunate perhaps that it was not part of the sunny festivities of a June Commencement, for one can imagine the frail-appearing, white-haired Mrs. Stone listening carefully to her citation, thanking the esteemed gentlemen Regents graciously, then at once launching into an address on the newest cause for which she was working: that women be appointed to the faculty of the University.

A few days after the telegram had arrived announcing her degree, Lucinda Stone was writing President Angell about

> a plan that I have much at heart and which I am anxious to see *materialize* during my lifetime as far as possible also in this our decadal year, which is to see founded and endowed a professorship in our University to be filled by a woman. Believing as I do most heartily in coeducation it seems to me a part of it.

Would President Angell approve, she asked, of her endeavor to

> raise $150,000 to endow a professorship of Social Science and Ethics, to be held by a woman professor. I want the sum to be contributed by the women of Michigan . . . Hitherto there have not been women prepared to fill such a position, but I am sure such are now to be found.[2]

Evidently she already had her eye on potential donors for a large proportion of that needed sum, for she speaks of "some friends of this new measure."

A few months later she was writing the Board of Regents, arguing her point:

> Women should not have been permitted to learn the alphabet if further demands were to be denied them . . . I now see and feel that an institution is not really coeducational until it is coeducating. Until men and women both and together form the teaching force and influence of that institution. Until the girls in the University can be brought into association with superior, cultivated, scholarly, accomplished women in the faculty of teachers, as well as men of the same grade of scholarly attainments . . . As men and women differ in their methods of doing intellectual work, education must of necessity be one-sided in which the teaching is done entirely by either men or women alone.[3]

Lucinda Stone was, however, a highly practical woman, perfectly aware of practical limitations. She knew the University was perennially short of money; she knew that men on the faculty would bitterly resent a woman occupying a position a man might fill. In explaining her proposal to raise money to endow special professorships for women, she made it clear:

> It is not proposed to displace any male member of the faculty, but to ask, if we will pay their salaries, may not some of the additional professors consequently required be women?

It was indeed a humble request—but there could be no other in view of the attitudes of that day. By 1890 there were able women scholars, of as high a calibre as men. What Lucinda Stone asked was only that the University hire the best women scholars, if the women of Michigan would agree to pay their salaries.

Three years later—in 1893—women would buy their way into Johns Hopkins Medical School in a similar way by offering an endowment of several hundred thousand dollars if the School would waive its restrictions on sex.[4]

Very probably the donors Lucinda Stone thought she could tap for the endowment fund were two members of the Board of Regents—Levi Louis Barbour and Charles Hebard.

In June of 1894 Barbour rose in the Regents' meeting to read aloud a memorial signed by 135 seniors and graduate students, asking that in all future appointments, women be given representation on the faculties of all departments of the University.

Barbour followed the memorial by proposing a remarkable resolution, which was unanimously adopted:

> Resolved, That henceforth in the selection of professors and instructors and other assistants in instruction in the University, no discrimination be made in selection between men and women, but that the applicant best fitted for the position receive the appointment.[5]

It was in all probability the first legal implementation in any university of an equal hiring policy for men and women. Two years later Dr. Eliza Mosher became the first woman to serve as full professor. As early as 1878 a young woman, Louisa Stowell, had been hired as Assistant in Microscopic Botany, followed by Dr.

Lena Leland in 1881 as Assistant Demonstrator in Anatomy, but neither of them had faculty status. Eliza Mosher was the first woman to sit in the faculty senate.

Whether women could or should teach on coeducational faculties was very much in the air in the mid-nineties. In June of 1896, just before Eliza Mosher took office, *The Castalian*, the annual publication of campus independents, surveyed presidents of coeducational colleges and universities on the question of women faculty members. President George A. Gates of Iowa College was

> surprised to learn that there is no woman on the faculty of Michigan. It does not seem to me logical that women should receive highest scholastic degrees and then be denied the natural and legitimate use of them.[6]

There were three or four women on the faculty of Iowa College, he added.

Most of the college presidents reflected, however, the kind of opinion and prejudice that had been voiced twenty-five years earlier against the acceptance of women as students. Thus President David Starr Jordan of Leland Stanford, while declaring that "intellect knows no sex," believed that "women will be admitted to the faculties of the American universities when they are as well prepared for the work as the men with whom they are to compete."

The president of Wisconsin, C. K. Adams, thought that while women made excellent teachers in the elementary grades, "it often happens that they lack either the physical vigor or the impelling ambition to rise into the higher ranges of professorial work." Henry Wade Rogers of Northwestern frankly pointed to the

> very strong prejudices that exist against the appointment of women professors . . . in the public mind, in the governing boards of the universities, among the faculties, and among the students. There is an impression that to make such appointments at all general would be to lower the tone and standing of the institutions which should enter on such a policy.

President R. H. Jesse declared that at Missouri State "we have hitherto found the men better qualified." He pointed out that women must make a choice early in life between career and marriage, that most chose the latter. He did not think that unmarried women could make successful teachers, for "premeditated abstinence from love and marriage . . . is apt to sterilize the heart and thus to spoil life." He did not indicate whether unmarried male teachers were disqualified by sterilized hearts.

Even President Angell was cautious in his remarks, while declaring himself in favor of

> appointing a certain number of women as teachers in colleges and universities which receive students of both sexes. No one can doubt that there are women who have the requisite scholarship for giving instruction in such institutions . . . Long ago in the Italian universities learned women demonstrated their fitness for professorial chairs.

He echoed the point Lucinda Stone had stressed of the importance of women professors as models and as sympathetic counsellors to women students. But he was careful to hedge on the numbers:

> At the same time I think that the number of women who should be called to chairs in our colleges and universities should be limited, and that most of the professors should be men.

When the pressing necessity for a women's gymnasium arose in 1893, Lucinda Stone apparently had to abandon her hope of raising $150,000 to endow a chair for a woman professor and turn her attention instead to the Women's Building fund. But in hundreds of letters, in personal calls on influential people, in speeches before women's groups throughout Michigan, in articles she wrote for the daily and weekly press, Lucinda Stone continued to press her point for hiring of women on the Michigan faculty.

When she died in 1900, the endowment had not been raised, but she had lived to see Eliza Mosher a full professor, and twelve other women serving in minor positions ranging from instructor down to Demonstrator of Nervous Diseases and Electro Therapeutics. They made up less than 5 percent of the faculty, but it is notable that, according to the Regents' records, there was no discrimination in the salaries paid to men and to women.

Eliza Mosher got the princely salary of $2000 a year—precisely the same as other full professors in the Medical Department and somewhat less than professors in the Literary Department where she was actually teaching, since it was assumed that teaching physicians earned extra emoluments from their part-time private practices. There was a good bit of criticism over her salary. Men in the lower professorial ranks saw no reason why Eliza Mosher should have the status and pay of a full professor, while they remained associates and assistants. Some faculty wives grumbled publicly about a single woman receiving more pay than faculty men with wives and families—though the same argument had apparently never been raised against single men on the faculty, who were numerous enough to form their own club, the Apostles.

In any case Lucinda Stone's idea had been planted.

In 1899 Mrs. Catherine Neafie Kellogg gave $10,000 for a chair in the University to be filled by "a woman of acknowledged ability" —in any field. The endowment had to be increased to $100,000— most of which was raised by Michigan alumnae—before Professor Helen Peak of the Psychology Department was named the first holder of the chair in 1955. Professor Elizabeth Douvan, also in the Psychology Department, now holds the chair.

After Alice Freeman Palmer's death in 1902, her husband, George Herbert Palmer, set up a trust fund to endow a chair in history in his wife's name in the University, to be held by a woman. She was to be "chosen on the same grounds of scholarship and general distinction in the field of research and teaching as apply in the selection of incumbents of other professorships," and should receive a salary "not less than the average paid other full professors in the Literary College."[7]

Not until 1957 was it possible, thanks to another legacy and to the additional funds raised by alumnae, to invite Dr. Caroline Robbins, Chairman of the History Department at Bryn Mawr, to hold the Alice Freeman Palmer professorship for the first time. At the present time Professor Sylvia Thrupp, noted medieval scholar, holds the Palmer chair.

Lucinda Stone's optimistic prediction of 1895 is still a long way from realization. She had looked forward to a day when

> the world has grown wiser as to these things, as it is fast growing wiser . . . the State will make appropriations for the support of women professors in some proportion as the number of young women in the University bears to that of the young men . . . and finally, that the thing once established, it will seem, like the admission of women students to the University, the most just and natural thing in the world."[8]

Women Earning Medical Degrees 1870 to 1970

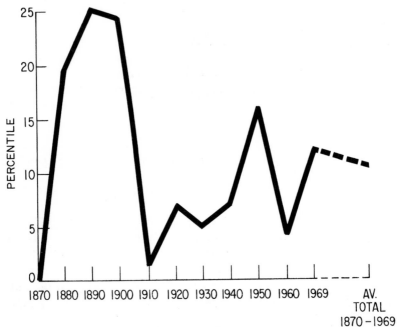

The proportion of women to men in medical classes in the University has fallen from 25 per cent to approximately 10 per cent.

12

Dr. Alice Hamilton and the "Dangerous Trades"

"The exercise of vital powers along lines of excellence in a life affording them scope" is an old Greek definition of happiness.

—Edith Hamilton, *The Greek Way*

One of the first persons in the United States to concern themselves with the effect of environmental pollution on the lives of human beings was Dr. Alice Hamilton, an 1893 graduate of the University of Michigan Medical School. Until her death in September of 1970 at 101 years old, Dr. Alice Hamilton had been the oldest living graduate of the University—and certainly one of the most remarkable.

In 1910 Alice Hamilton, a slender, pretty, hazel-eyed woman with the soft voice and charming manners of careful breeding, set out on a trek across the country that took her into factories, plants, workshops where no woman had ever stepped before, where men shovelled deadly poisonous white lead carbonate amid noxious clouds, where men scraped and breathed in flaking paint from the ceilings of pullman cars, where men enamelled bathtubs, polished cut glass, "turned" coffins, wrapped cigars in tinfoil—and sickened and died of diseases no doctor could diagnose, no hospital could cure.

"Strange business for a woman," said a miner in an Arizona copper mine, when Alice Hamilton descended into the precarious tunnels to observe men using the jack hammer, and to see for herself whether copper dust might be causing the high incidence of miners' tuberculosis.[1]

Alice Hamilton's whole life would be devoted to her investigation of "the dangerous trades", of the perils that lurked in hundreds of industries in a day when no laws protected the workingman or woman from occupational disease—and when no insurance compensated them or their families if they fell ill and died. ("There is something strange," Dr. Hamilton thought, "in speaking of 'accident and sickness compensation,' " for what could compensate anyone for loss of health or loss of life?)

Of her investigations Alice Hamilton wrote:

> It was pioneering, exploration of an unknown field. No young doctor nowadays can hope for work as exciting and rewarding. Everything I discovered was new and most of it was really valuable.[2]

Fifty years earlier, Alice Hamilton could not have had a college education.

Born in 1869, the year before women were admitted to Michigan, daughter of a well-to-do Fort Wayne family, she grew up in those decades of the late nineteenth century when it appeared to educated women that all the doors of the larger world were indeed opening to them.

As it has for generations of women students—even more than for men—the University gave Alice Hamilton her first experience of personal freedom:

> Ann Arbor gave me my first taste of emancipation and I loved it. I loved to feel that nobody was worrying about me when I came back late from the library, nobody even knew when I came.

In spite of the still segregated anatomy classes and certain others (as the University catalog stated, "lectures and demonstrations which it is not desirable to present to the two sexes together") Alice Hamilton looked back on her studies at the University as "happy and exciting years":

> The school was coeducational and had been so for some twenty years, so we women were taken for granted and

there was none of the sex antagonism which I saw later in Eastern schools.[3]

A little later, after a year's interneship at the New England Hospital for Women and Children, one of the few hospitals which accepted women internes, Alice and her sister Edith—who was to become the world-renowned Greek scholar—travelled to Germany for a year's study. The all-male German universities in the 1890's were at exactly the point, insofar as admitting women was concerned, where American universities had been in the 1860's:

Even gaining permission to study in one of the German universities was a long and difficult enterprise, for of course women were not admitted to any of them.

The Hamilton sisters—one in medicine, one in classics—attended lectures at the Universities of Leipzig and Munich just as Alice Boise had attended classes at Michigan in 1866—"invisibly". They too had to make their way, as Madelon Stockwell had, through a crowd of young men students who gathered to stare at the audacious foreign women.

Alice Hamilton remarked philosophically of that year:

It is not for a woman who has been on the faculty at Harvard to be too derisive about German universities in the nineties.

And she added:

When German universities did admit women, they went the whole way—no dormitories, no rules, no Dean of Women, the same freedom for women students as for men.[4]

While Michigan had followed the pattern of German universities earlier in the nineteenth century, now German universities followed that of Michigan.

A few years earlier, one of Alice Hamilton's professors, Dr. Albert Prescott, in recommending her for an internship, had written of her "somewhat severe distrust of her own abilities," as well as her "unconscious spirit of helpfulness."[5]

Both traits were characteristic of that early generation of college-trained women. Women's brains were not yet a commodity valued or sought after in the marketplace; many, perhaps all, were troubled by self-doubt.

But they did share a deep sense of concern for problems of social welfare, a concern that was part of the whole Progressive impulse of the 1880's and '90's. Not until the 1960's would a generation of young Americans again commit themselves so eagerly to changing society for the better.

After her return from Europe and a year of additional study at Johns Hopkins—which had just opened its doors to women—Alice Hamilton made the most decisive move of her life. She had heard Jane Addams speak in Fort Wayne just before she had left for Germany. Though in after years she could not recall a word of that speech, it had moved her so deeply that Alice Hamilton determined she would one day live in Hull House.

The famous settlement house which Jane Addams founded in the Chicago slum area in 1889 was one of the first and by far the most influential of American settlement houses. In the closing years of the nineteenth century those settlement houses—with their day care centers for working mothers, their baby clinics, and their classes and lectures for adults—drew thousands of young, idealistic, middle-class women to devote their energies to the problems of the very poor. The leaders of the movement—women like Jane Addams, Lillian Wald, Florence Kelley—provided the first heroic models of women in public life.

To newly-emancipated young women a concern for the problems of the larger community seemed a natural extension of the age-old feminine capacity for nurturing; human society was envisioned as a natural extension of the family. When Jane Addams wrote and spoke—as she did in Ann Arbor in 1896—she urged women to take on their consciences the welfare of the larger neighborhood:

> As society grows more complicated, it is necessary that woman shall extend her sense of responsibility to many things outside of her own home, if only in order to preserve the home in its entirety.[6]

Alice Hamilton moved into Hull House in 1898 and made it her home until 1919. While she taught pathology classes at the Woman's Medical College of Northwestern University during the day, she worked nights and weekends among the immigrant poor in the slum quarter that surrounded Hull House. She learned first-hand the problems of working people—unprotected in that day by unions and labor legislation.

When she faced a choice between a career of laboratory research and one of more immediate service to human beings, she could choose her direction without hesitation:

> I shall always be thankful for the training in scientific
> method I had . . . but I never have doubted the wisdom
> of my decision to give it up and devote myself to work
> which has been scientific only in part, but human and
> practical in greater measure.[7]

In August of 1914 Alice Hamilton was about to sail from Montreal to Europe to study the protection of workers in lead factories in England and Germany.

As William O'Neill writes, "Women had long thought of themselves as uniquely pacific in temper."[8] Women's organizations had already formed their peace departments in the nineteenth century, and many women leaders were active pacifists. Though suffrage had not yet been won except in scattered states, intelligent women like Jane Addams and Alice Hamilton thought the eventual influence of women in public life would certainly lead to the abolition of force as an instrument of policy.

The outbreak of hostilities in 1914 was an especially severe shock to women pacifists. As early as the fall of 1914 a group formed the Women's Peace Party, and in April of 1915 Alice Hamilton accompanied Jane Addams to war-torn Europe to attend the first International Congress of Women in The Hague. Women leaders from twelve neutral and warring nations met not only to protest but to search out a practical means of ending the war at once.

At first the 50 American delegates on board ship were, wrote Dr. Hamilton, like a "perpetual meeting of the Woman's City Club or the Federation of Settlements." But before long she could write:

> We have long passed the state of poems, and impassioned
> appeals and 'messages from womankind' and willing-
> ness to die in the cause, and now we are discovering
> whether it is more dangerous to insist on democratic
> control of diplomacy than it is to insist on the neutrali-
> zation of the seas.[9]

It was the American group who devised the practical plan, later adopted by the Women's Congress, of "continuous mediation" for the settlement of the war by a group of statesmen from neutral nations under the initiative of the United States, who were to recommend solutions and alternatives to the belligerents until the fighting halted—hopefully before any decisive military victory was achieved.

The women's plan, though widely praised and more widely supported than any other, was not implemented even by the United States, which gradually drifted into the war.

Four years later, in 1919, many of the same women met again, this time in Zurich, for the Second International Congress of Women. The delegates—representing defeated as well as victorious and neutral nations—hoped they could bring their weight to bear for a just peace on the men meeting at Versailles to write the treaty. When the terms of the treaty were made public, the Women's Congress in Zurich was the first group to scrutinize the peace terms and to condemn them as seriously violating "the principles upon which alone a just and lasting peace can be secured, and which the democracies of the world can come to accept."[10]

The allied press denounced the resolutions of the Women's Congress with great vehemence; only gradually, as months and years passed, did students of international affairs begin to agree with the resolutions the women had passed in Zurich in 1919.

On her return to the United States at the conclusion of the Congress, Alice Hamilton was invited to become the first woman to teach at Harvard University. She was to be Assistant Professor of Industrial Medicine, and although she was already a world-renowned authority in her field, she was hired at precisely the same salary the University of Michigan had paid Eliza Mosher twenty-five years earlier. Alice Hamilton was asked moreover never to insist on her right to use the Harvard Club, nor to demand her quota of football tickets; and though she would receive the formal engraved invitation issued to all Harvard faculty to march in the academic procession at Commencement, the warning always appeared across her invitation that "under no circumstances may a woman sit on the platform."

When newspaper reporters came to interview Dr. Hamilton on her dazzling new appointment, she answered her questioners briefly:

> "Yes, I am the first woman on the Harvard faculty. I'm not the first woman who should have been appointed."[11]

13

Two Steps Back in the 1900's:
Reaction Against Coeducation

There, little girl, don't read,
You're fond of your books, I know,
But Brother might mope
If he had no hope
Of getting ahead of you.
It's dull for a boy who cannot lead
There, little girl, don't read.[1]

—Alice Duer Miller, 1915

There had been no doubt something of naivete' in the bright optimism with which the first generations of college-bred women faced their opening horizons, in the confidence they felt in their new liberty, in their faith that intelligent, dedicated women might join forces with intelligent, dedicated men to solve the world's problems.

Having won the right to decide how and where they were to be educated, they imagined they had also won the right to choose their professions, to decide whether they would or would not marry, whether they would bear children, and if so, how many. Although the vote was not yet theirs, most women were confident it soon would be—and with it the opportunity to participate as fellow human beings in the decision-making processes of a democratic society.

Events did not quite work out that way. In very important ways the year 1900 proved to be the high-water mark of women's achievements for the next half-century.

Occupations that were sex-segregated in 1900 remained so. Although two world wars would send women temporarily into previously male jobs, in the long run no new occupations were opened to women. In certain professions, such as medicine, where women had made substantial headway, the proportion of women entering began to decline.

While the exceptional few graduates found comparatively well-paying jobs on college faculties, by far the greater number of women—even armed with their Bachelor's degrees and their teacher's diplomas certifying their "special fitness for teaching"—faced low-paying, low-status jobs in elementary and secondary schools. When the Association of Collegiate Alumnae surveyed the earnings of their teaching members, only about one-fifth reported earning enough to support eventual retirement.

After the first great progress made by coeducation in the 1870's and 1880's, when Michigan, Cornell and most large universities in the Midwest and Far West opened their doors to women, there had been a lull. Eastern men's colleges did not follow the lead of Cornell and the midwestern universities but adopted instead the principle of "annexes" or "coordinate" women's colleges. Thus Radcliffe grew out of the Society for the Collegiate Instruction of Women, established in 1882, with Harvard faculty members teaching women separately, and without granting Harvard degrees. For nearly half a century Radcliffe women had no access, or at most very limited access, to the rich resources of the Harvard library. Barnard, coordinate of Columbia, provided certain additional advantages to women students from the beginning—they might have access to the Columbia Library, and they might earn Columbia degrees. Pembroke College, coordinate of Brown, was set up along similar lines in 1891.

Not until the nineteen-fifties would any additional all-male universities—such as the University of Michigan had been until 1870—open their doors to women.

The reaction against the women's movement was first discernible in the very area where women had first struggled to win acceptance: in the area of higher education.

Beginning in the early 1900's a number of previously coeducational colleges began a policy of segregating women from men—

at least in certain areas or departments—and of applying a quota system to limit the numbers of women who might enter.

That the move toward segregation was a regressive measure was perfectly clear to alert women at the time. In some places, as at the University of Chicago, alumnae groups protested vigorously. Women were aware then and later that segregated facilities rarely provided equal educational opportunities for the disadvantaged group against whom the measures were directed.

The chief reason for that reaction against coeducation in the early 1900's was simply the tremendous increase in the numbers of women seeking higher education in the closing years of the nineteenth century. While the overall numbers of both men and women enrolled had climbed astronomically between 1870 and 1900, the proportion of women to men in the college population had shown the sharpest increase.

By 1900 the enrollment of women in American colleges and universities had soared to over 100,000—and of these 70 per cent were enrolled in coeducational institutions.

At Michigan the proportion of women students had increased from 3 per cent in 1871 to 22 per cent of the student body. In the Literary Department the proportion was about 47 per cent, and, as President Angell told the Regents, more women than men were finishing college, for in 1899 53 per cent of all Bachelor of Arts degrees went to women.

At some universities, such as Chicago and Stanford, the proportion of women to men was even higher. At Oberlin women constituted 53 per cent of the students; at the Universities of Minnesota and California they made up a majority in the literary departments.

The fear began to be openly expressed by all-male administrations that at least some of their departments were in grave danger of being "feminized."

James Rowland Angell, son of Michigan's President and a Professor of Psychology at the University of Chicago, where agitation to separate men from women was underway, described in a perceptive article in 1902 the rising attack on coeducation:

> [The woman student] has recently shown a disposition
> to outnumber the young men in her classes, and this
> is resented by certain of her mentors as an obvious
> impropriety. The occasion has been seized upon by

reactionaries here and there to magnify the drawbacks of coeducation.[2]

The original argument against the admission of women to the universities had been on the ground of intellectual incapacity. But women had proven beyond any doubt that they could hold their own academically.

At Michigan a chapter of Phi Beta Kappa was established in 1907—belatedly, compared to other universities of similar prestige, because Michigan still used a no-grading system, which made selection of top students difficult. When a chapter was established, a faculty committee designated the outstanding scholars of the senior class in the Literary College. In 1907 three women and five men were chosen; in 1908, 13 women and 11 men; in 1909, 11 women and 19 men; and in 1910, 21 women and 15 men; during all these years women were a minority of the Literary Department enrollment. It did appear that brains were without gender.[3]

Now the original argument of intellectual inferiority was reversed, and it was claimed that male students were being forced into unfair competition, that the presence of large numbers of women, especially in the literary departments, was driving away men students.

Angell in his article proceeded to review and to refute all the old arguments against coeducation that were being dusted off and refurbished by coeducation's latest critics. The charge that the presence of women caused "a blight upon college spirit" Angell dismissed as the "most fatuous" complaint. Others thought women "exercise a deleterious effect on that impalpable something known as academic atmosphere"—a certain something peculiar to Oxford, Yale, and Harvard. Some complained that the social proprieties were being violated; others thought that women in coeducational colleges suffered "a loss of refinement and feminine nicety."

But the basic criticism levelled by the anti-coeducators was simply that there were too many women going to college, that they were crowding men students out of certain areas—especially English, history, modern languages and classical studies. On the other hand, men remained in overwhelming majority in law, medicine, technology, mathematics and the exact sciences. Critics of coeducation argued that this disposition of the sexes to choose different academic areas proved the existence of "sex in mind," and that therefore there should be separate and quite different education for men and women.

Angell in his article pointed out that young people chose their college courses "from the earliest possible moment in such a manner as most effectively to assist in the preparation for a professional career." Virtually the only careers open to women were teaching and medicine; teaching jobs available to women were almost entirely in secondary schools—and even there, chiefly in English and the humanities—which explained their choice of these subjects in college. He pointed out, in addition, that girls were conditioned from childhood "to cultivate a mild but definite variety of sentimentalism," and "that which passes as native taste is itself often a mere expression of social and domestic pressure, emphasizing with relentless insistence certain interests as sexually appropriate or practically valuable."

A few years before Angell's article in defense of coeducation, one of the first open attacks on coeducation—and an unusually virulent one—had appeared in the University of Michigan literary magazine, *The Inlander*. It was written by a prominent alumnus, a Detroit lawyer, Albert Jacobs, A.B. '73, LL.B. '76. Jacobs' article made use of many of the arguments against coeducation which Angell later quoted, averring that the growing enrollment of women had reduced the number of men students at Michigan, had lowered the prestige of the University, and cost it valuable financial aid from alumni.

Tracing the course of the University since the admission of women, Jacobs wrote:

> Graduates and undergraduates of other colleges spoke of Michigan very differently in 1876 from the manner of speaking in 1870. The overwhelming sentiment of college men, at least of those residing in the large cities was and is against coeducation, and the University suffered, still suffers in consequence . . . The enrollment in the University just before the admission of women was 1,111. In the year following the attendance it was 1,110, of whom 31 were women, a loss of 32 men. In 1876-77, seven years after coeducation began, we find 1,110 students and of these 97 women, so the loss in men was 98.[4]

Jacobs went on to declare that the presence of women students at Michigan simply made it less desirable to males citing "the general opinion of college men that a coeducational institution is presumptively inferior":

> Oberlin has for half a century given instruction to all, irrespective of sex or color; but her liberality does not render her more attractive than Yale, from which women are excluded, or than the University of Virginia where Negroes cannot enter.

Jacobs deplored the decrease in college spirit; men just weren't having as much fun as they had had before women entered:

> [Coeducation] destroys the conditions essential to the development of a distinctive college life . . . At Ann Arbor [in 1869] a peculiar, an interesting student life was forming. Within a few years all the old usages and celebrations disappeared . . . Commencement dinners are distinctly less enjoyable of late years than they used to be.

But Jacobs' chief argument against coeducation—and in favor of changing the University's policy to segregation—was that women graduates did not bestow the financial benefits that male graduates did:

> We might admit that one Minnie or Nellie is more useful to the University than a plain John or Thomas; but we are not sure that one Minnie or Nellie is likely, all things considered, to help the University as much in after life as two Johns or two Thomases would. These Johns and Thomases have a habit of subscribing to gymnasium funds, and of voting legislative appropriations.

While agreeing that "the women of Michigan are entitled to receive from the State an education as complete and as cheap as the State furnishes to men," nevertheless, thought Jacobs—and many others with him—

> no law requires that they shall be educated together with men. Let the Regents and the State make separate provision for the instruction of the 350 women now in the Literary Department. Let the female students be organized into a college by themselves . . . Little trouble and hardly any additional expense would be occasioned by a division on the line of sex.

Jacobs was certainly quite right about the comparative economic power of men and women graduates. Men graduated to become businessmen, lawyers, engineers; women graduated to become secondary school teachers, wives and mothers. Nevertheless, interestingly enough, in the very decade during which Jacobs wrote his scathing indictment of coeducation, the first large bequest came to the University—and it came from a woman, Dr. Elizabeth Bates of Port Chester, New York. Dr. Bates left her entire estate of $100,000 to the University of Michigan, to establish a professorship in the Diseases of Women and Children, because it was the first university to open its medical school to women.

Jacobs' arguments might have been dismissed as superficial and his article of no importance, except that it revealed so deepseated a resentment against the presence of women at a large publicly-supported university, and presaged a reaction against coeducation that was soon well underway.

In addition to the argument that women were intellectually inferior, the second argument against coeducation had been on the ground of women's health: that their physical constitution would be damaged by higher education and especially the coeducational variety. Although educators such as President Angell and the heads of the women's colleges had refuted the statement repeatedly, declaring the health of their women students was above, not below, the general level, now the thesis was given a new twist, and one much harder to refute.

It was now argued that higher education damaged the breeding function of American women, that college women were marrying later and producing fewer children. The new fear, rooted in a reactionary political climate and openly expressed in numerous publications of the time, was that the higher education of women was endangering the supremacy of the Anglo-Saxon, native-born ruling class in America.

What alarmed conservative-minded social scientists in the early 1900's was the revelation that the great influx of immigrants were producing nearly twice as many children as native-born middle class women. Theodore Roosevelt, branding the practice of contraception as "frightful and fundamental immorality," predicted that unless "the old native American stock" increased its birthrate, the American people would be committing "race suicide."[5]

Physicians, scientists, social scientists, deploring the falling birth rate of middle class America, tied it to the "emancipated" woman—and especially the college-educated woman. All the surveys showed that college-educated women were indeed marrying later and in fewer numbers, and producing fewer children than the general population.

The British Darwinist, Herbert Spencer, with the straightest of straight scientific faces, deduced from the facts

> that absolute or relative infertility is commonly produced in women by mental labour carried to excess . . . the deficiency of reproductive power among [upperclass girls] may be reasonably attributed to the overtaxing of their brains.[6]

Dr. G. Stanley Hall, psychologist and President of Clark University, condemned higher education for women at the National Education Association conference in 1903, on the same ground:

> The first danger to woman is over-brainwork. It affects that part of her organism which is sacred to heredity. This danger is seen in the diminishing number of marriages. The postponement of marriage is very unfortunate in its influence upon civilization.[7]

In his influential work, *Adolescence,* published in 1904, Dr. Hall reviewed in detail the literature of the previous 30 years on the relationship of education to women's health. He concluded:

> that the more scholastic the education of women, the fewer children and the harder, more dangerous and more dreaded the parturition, and the less the ability to nurse children. Not intelligence but education by present man-made ways is inversely as fecundity. . . . Mere learning is not the ideal, and prodigies of scholarship are always morbid. The rule should be to keep nothing that is not to become practical; not to overburden the soul with the impedimenta of libraries and records of what is afar off in time.[8]

Hall thought ideally girls should be segregated in schools completely devoted to their preparation for motherhood, with plain cooking, plenty of sleep, exercise, emphasis on manners and religion. Religion, he explained, occupied the place in a woman's life that politics did in a man's.

Dr. Hall quite obviously saw eye to eye with his mentor, Sigmund Freud, whom he brought to the United States in 1909 for the single, one-week visit the Viennese founder of psychoanalysis ever spent in the United States.

Freud himself, who challenged so many shibboleths of Victorian thinking, never challenged the mid-nineteenth century sexual status quo, in which he himself had been reared. In an interview in 1935 Freud condemned the American system of coeducation, blamed coeducated women for the high divorce rate, labeled American women—of whom he certainly knew very few— "an anti-cultural phenomenon. They have nothing but conceit to make up for their sense of uselessness."[9]

Nor did Freud ever perceive any parallel between his position as a member of the Jewish minority in central Europe—though he would suffer bitterly for it—and the disadvantaged position of women in society. Others had drawn the parallel, and there had been in nineteenth-century Hungary a movement aiming at "civil rights for Jews and women," analagous to the thrust in America for civil rights for blacks and women.

Like Sigmund Freud, most male opinion-makers in early twentieth-century America—men like G. Stanley Hall, Grover Cleveland, Woodrow Wilson—had been conditioned by mid-Victorian ideas and myths of woman's place in society.

In the half century since the movement for women's rights had begun, many women—especially educated women—had come to hold a very different view of themselves than their mothers and grandmothers had. With social independence they had gained self-confidence, a sense of individual worth. Many thousands were self-supporting; one in every six women worked in paid employment by 1900. Large numbers had proved that their brains as well as their sex might be put to use for the benefit of society.

The door that Nora slammed on her doll's house in an Oslo theatre in 1879 had echoed across the stages of two continents.

It was inevitable that woman's newer view of herself would conflict with those who held the older masculine views of "woman's sphere." Some men even felt as strongly as a learned professor acquaintance of James Rowland Angell, who proposed "an uprising of men to force by violence a return of women to their proper sphere."[10]

Others, like Grover Cleveland, simply did not approve of women's desire to vote.

One of Michigan's early graduates, Lucy Salmon, who did advanced graduate work under History Professor Woodrow Wilson at Bryn Mawr, recollected that "he never whole-heartedly believed in college education for women . . . He always assumed that they were intellectually different from men and that, therefore, they would not interest him."[11]

While there were men like the two Angells, father and son, who continued to defend coeducation, who continued to regard women as individuals with individual brains, talents and potential to contribute to society, they were very much a minority in the early 1900's.

Already when the younger Angell wrote his defence of coeducation in 1902, his own University of Chicago had begun to reverse its coeducational policy, which had from its founding offered "opportunities for all departments of higher education to persons of both sexes on equal terms." According to Thomas Woody, when a large endowment was tentatively dangled, provided that women were segregated from men, the Chicago administration in a fairly high-handed way, began to separate the sexes for at least the first two years:

> The work of segregation will be gradual, but when it has been completed, men and women will never meet in class, at lectures, or at chapel.[12]

In actual fact Chicago did not carry its segregation policy very far, but the threat to the principle of coeducation remained. Western Reserve decided to segregate, despite opposition from students; Tufts in Massachussetts and the University of Rochester set up separate women's colleges.

Other universities adopted a somewhat different policy and began to segregate individual classes and courses, especially in literary departments, in the hope of boosting male enrollment.

At Wisconsin, where in 1906 women constituted 50.8 per cent of the student body, President Van Hise arranged separate classes for men and women in the liberal arts, on the ground that "humanistic studies . . . are chosen by women in such numbers that men desert them almost entirely." He did not agree with Angell that academic choice was a result of occupational direction, but that something called "natural segregation of the sexes" led to men's pre-empting "colleges of engineering, law, commerce, agriculture and medicine," while women concentrated in "such courses as home economics, household science or domestic science." The Universities of Kansas and Washington also adopted a policy of separate classes for the two sexes.[13]

Other colleges and universities began to practice a quota system, limiting entirely the number of women admitted. Stanford announced it would admit no more than 500 women henceforth. Wesleyan limited women to 20 per cent, later eliminated them entirely.

Numerous publicly-supported colleges and universities would practice an informal quota system, whereby admissions officers restricted the number of women entering, as many did the numbers of Jewish students, often by applying substantially higher entrance qualifications for women than for men.

A few voices protested the new policies of segregation and limitation. The former President of Wisconsin and an ardent supporter of coeducation, Dr. John Bascom, deplored the reactionary trend, foreseeing that "this attitude is sure, sooner or later . . . to issue in a course fitted, according to someone's notion, for women, and less comprehensive than the course designed for men . . . till we reach courses which exclude women from the freest and most profitable forms of study."[14]

President Angell, recognizing the dangers in even so liberal a university as Michigan, promised in April of 1908 that Michigan would never retrench on its policy of admitting women equally with men:

> The burden of proof [he wrote] is on those who propose segregation and I know of no sufficient arguments to sustain their proposition. We have never thought for a moment of resorting to it here.[15]

But after the passing of Angell, perhaps even in his last years, Michigan too became less liberal in its policies toward women. Michigan joined other colleges in practicing a quota system on the admission of women, defending the practice in a variety of ingenious ways.

As late as the 1920's President Clarence Little thought women should follow a different group of studies from men—physiology, nursing hygiene, human behavior, heredity and genetics, that would prepare them primarily for the role of homemakers and mothers.[16]

The pattern of discrimination against women continued for at least a half century.

The University Club for faculty members did not include women serving on the faculty. The Research Club, founded in 1900 "to unite those members of the academic staff who are actively engaged in research," excluded women until the 1950's, did not even invite Edith Hamilton, the renowned Greek scholar when she taught on campus.

Women, like second-class citizens in colonial empires, entered the Michigan Union by the side door only.

Old prejudices, old prerogatives lingered on: those habits of thought that Virginia Woolf labelled "tough as roots but intangible as sea-mist."

14

Revolution in Slow Motion

When men and women are prevented from recognizing one another's essential humanity by sexual prejudices, nourished by legal as well as social institutions, society as a whole remains less than it could otherwise become.

—Leo Kanowitz, *Women and the Law*[1]

"A radical revolution," Michigan's second President, the Reverend Erastus Haven, called the risky idea of admitting women to the University in 1867. And, to be sure, he was right. But neither Erastus Haven, nor anyone else in his day, had any vision of just how radical would be the changes in the lives of women over the next hundred years.

Madelon Stockwell, the first woman student, born in 1845, spanned in the eight decades of her life the most revolutionary of those events — changes that would affect more human lives in more profound ways than any revolution in human history.

The major changes in the fabric of women's lives were gifts of science and were these: for the first time in history women could bear only children they chose to bear, could hope to survive the process of childbirth, could hope to see the children they bore grow to maturity. For the first time in history women had the same potential for autonomy over their lives as men.

When Madelon Stockwell was born, a girl child could expect to live to the age of forty and a half years old. If she married at the usual age and was fertile, she could expect to be involved in childbearing up to the day of her death—and might very likely die of the process itself. If she were lucky enough to survive the hazards of many pregnancies and many childbirths, she could expect to see as many as half the children she bore die before they reached adulthood.

Madelon Stockwell was three years old when the first Women's Rights Convention was held at Seneca Falls. But already the previous year, in 1847, an event had occurred of greater import to women throughout the world than the publication of the Declaration of Sentiments. That year an obscure young Hungarian obstetrician named Ignaz Semmelweiss, concerned at the fearful death toll among women in the lying-in wards of Vienna's great General Hospital—anywhere from 8 to 16 per cent of women in labor—deduced the cause of puerperal fever as infection from the unclean hands of medical students coming from the autopsy rooms. Semmelweiss introduced asepsis in the practice of obstetrics, in a single year reduced the death toll to less than 1 per cent. He himself died a few years later, tragically unappreciated, insane,—died, ironically, of a dissection wound. But Semmelweiss' observation and concern saved the lives of countless thousands of child-bearing women from his time on.

Besides safer childbirth, the latter half of the nineteenth century saw the rapid spread of contraceptive knowledge and practice. The repressive Comstock Law of 1873, which defined contraceptive information as "obscene and lewd," followed by restrictive state laws—in a day when women had no vote—inhibited for half a century dissemination of birth control information. Nevertheless, family limitation began to be widely practiced, especially among the educated middle class—as the falling birth rate of college graduates in the United States clearly testified.

Although Grant Allen, writing as late as 1889, estimated that "about six children per marriage are necessary to keep up the population as more than one-half die before maturity," within a few years lifesaving medical advances reduced infant and child mortality.[2] Parents could have smaller families and hope to see their children live to survive them.

By 1900 American women had added 11 years to their life expectancy; by 1920, 20 additional years; and by the 1960's a girl child could count on living to the age of 74.7 years old—nearly double the life-span of a girl born in Madelon Stockwell's birth decade.

Besides the extension of women's lifetimes far beyond the

childbearing years, a final benefit bestowed by technology was the great simplification of housekeeping chores. The introduction of mechanical plumbing, of new ways of cooking and heating, the use of factory-processed foods and factory-made clothing, enormously eased the burden of household drudgery demanded of women in Madelon Stockwell's Victorian childhood.

By the time of World War I sexual mores too had begun to change—and to change far more dramatically for women than for men. Covertly at first, overtly after the war, women began to rebel against the double standard of moral behavior—rebelled by refusing to obey it. Kinsey's studies only bore out what the earlier studies of Gilbert Hamilton and Lewis M. Terman had shown—that the lives of women born after 1890, and even more significantly among those born after 1900, revealed a sharply-increased incidence of pre- and extra-marital sexual experience.

Western literature would have to abandon one of its favorite themes—theme of the most outrageous comedy, the most searing tragedy from Chaucer to Tolstoy: the efforts of fathers and husbands to enforce chastity as a kind of property insurance, and the efforts of women—and their lovers—to elude it.

And finally, as woman's right to make decisions in crucial areas of her private life appeared to approach realization, so did the right to participate in the decision-making processes of society. Well before her death in 1924 Madelon Stockwell could go to the polls and vote with other American women in a national presidential election. The first generation of college-trained women had contributed important leadership to the suffrage movement. Sarah Burger Stearns, the first girl to apply for admission to Michigan in the 1850's, had become a national leader in the movement. Michigan graduates Lucy Maynard Salmon, Octavia Bates, Cora Benneson, Sarah Dix Hamlin and many others, worked actively in the struggle that finally won the vote for women.

And so, after 1920—what then? Did women's life patterns change as openly and dramatically as those revolutionary changes promised? Did they at once invade the professions, "put heart into government"—as the suffragists had rosily promised?

The answer, of course, is no.

Rather astutely a young *Michigan Daily* writer, editorializing in 1920 on the eve of the suffrage amendment, foresaw that a change in the sexual status quo might well be as beneficial for men as for women:

> Now that the first apprehension which always follows
> upon indication of a radical social change has passed,
> men are coming to accept the movement of women to-
> ward an equal footing with them as natural, rather than
> monstrous or blasphemous. The most potent considera-
> tion in altering the masculine viewpoint is perhaps that
> man's superiority, once it is brought into the light of day
> and examined, appears to be a liability rather than the
> asset it has been considered heretofore.[3]

But few men were ready to shed blithely the old concepts of
men's and women's places in the scheme of things. Nor, probably,
were women. Victorian images of masculinity and femininity remained little modified. Still conditioned from childhood to think
of marriage as the single suitable occupation for the female adult,
women too were uncertain about how to live their new lives, how
to use the extra years granted them.

In a world still structured around nineteenth century concepts,
a career for a married woman usually meant the double burden of
outside work and household responsibilities. Housework has by no
means vanished even with mechanical tools; and a Department of
Agriculture study in 1929 showed that the average urban house-
wife worked about 50 hours a week at domestic chores. The figure
has changed little since then. The lack of public day nurseries,
moreover, has added to the hardship of working women with children.

A study of women appearing in *Who's Who in America* between
1920 and 1964 showed not only a decline in numbers of women
listed from 8.4 per cent to 4.4 per cent, but revealed that "of all
women listed, 40 per cent were unmarried and 41 per cent child-
less."[4]

If the pursuit of a career demanded the sacrifice of marriage and
family, it appeared that women would rather choose the Yeatsian
"perfection of the life than of the work."

If women were not electing professional careers, however, they
were taking jobs and working outside the home in increasing numbers. And the kinds of jobs they held, the amount of wages they
earned—like the extent to which they engaged actively in politics—
depended chiefly on one factor: education.

Within the University of Michigan the enrollment of women
increased from 28 per cent in 1920 to 37 per cent in 1930, and there
the proportion of women students has hovered for 40 years—except

for one period, when the number of women's admissions was sharply curtailed.

On the campus of the University, the living patterns of women students did not change to any marked degree after World War I. Academically they continued to do as well as, or a bit better than, men students. They wrote and acted in Junior Girls' Plays, sang in Choral Union, played in student orchestras, cheered at football games, danced in the Union on Friday and Saturday nights.

More of them lived in dormitories and sororities, some in the League houses that had the Dean's seal of approval. They may not have liked the rules that regulated the hours they kept, the lives they led, but, on the whole, they obeyed them.

From the beginning of women's entrance into higher education, it was apparent that most families were less ready to make sacrifices for their daughters' educations than for sons'. When President Angell surveyed the student body in 1906, he found more than one-fourth—women as well as men—working to earn part or all of their expenses. In 1912 at least 60 girls were earning board and room by doing housework, mending, caring for children and tutoring. It has usually been harder for women students to earn money then men. As college students they earn about one-third less—and are less apt to borrow for their education.[5]

In 1917 Michigan alumnae, who had previously been members of the Association of Collegiate Alumnae, formed their own separate organization under the Michigan Alumnae Council. Over the years they raised nearly a half million dollars in scholarships and fellowships, established the first cooperative houses for women students, were largely instrumental in building the Michigan League, the central club building for women students.

In 1917 too former Regent Levi Lewis Barbour, having been deeply impressed by the work of Michigan-trained women physicians in China and Japan, founded the Barbour Scholarships for Oriental Women. The Fund, now valued at more than $650,000, has brought several hundred women from China, Japan, and other parts of the East to Michigan; they have returned to their own countries to become physicians, teachers, college presidents.

If the over-all enrollment of women at Michigan remained largely unchanged for 50 years, the proportion of women on the University faculty actually decreased during the first decades of the century. Over and over again alumnae groups petitioned the Regents

The Center for Continuing Education of Women, founded in 1964, was one of the first in the country to aid women whose education has been interrupted. Nearly 3000 women have received advice and help on educational plans and jobs.

Mrs. Jean Campbell, Director of the Center, talks with one of the winners of the first C.C.E.W. fellowships for returning women, Mrs. Amanda Renshaw, Ph.D. candidate in astrophysics. (Photo by Lee.)

Mrs. Lorraine Autin, mother of five, drove a school bus to earn tuition costs for her return to college. (Photo by Lee.)

Mrs. Jane Bloom, mother of 10 children, is a student in the Medical School, expecting to specialize in pediatrics. (Photo by Abbey.)

Elistine Beall, Jane Bloom, Debbie Oakley, Jane Schultz returned to the University to earn advanced degrees in music education, medicine, public health, human genetics. (Detroit News Photo.)

Gail Walker, wife of a political scientist, mother of two, pursues research in social organization. (Photo by Lee.)

Mrs. Louise Cain, first Director of the Center, wrote the original proposal for the Center's founding in 1964.

Mrs. Irene Murphy, former Regent, was an early adviser of the Center.

Mrs. Lucy Miller backpacks 18-month-old Philip all around campus, says he loves campus life. She is one of the student wives and young mothers enrolled in the evening degree courses sponsored by the Center. (Photo by Lee.)

to appoint additional women to the faculty; proceedings of the Board report that the petitions were always "received and placed on file." Miss Alice Hunt, Instructor in Drawing from 1889 to 1919, taught generations of engineers and architects. During most of that time she was almost the only woman on the faculty, besides the Dean of Women and the instructors in physical education. When Alice Hunt retired in 1919, she was receiving top pay for an instructor—$1400—but in the entire span of her 30 years of teaching, she had never been given a single promotion.

In 1929, after long agitation by alumnae groups, the first woman Regent, Mrs. Esther Marsh Cram, '98, was appointed to fill a vacancy. Mrs. Cram was no feminist, and she hastened to assure her fellow Regents, "Gentlemen, I expect to be a woman Regent, not a women's Regent." There has been a woman Regent—never more than one—on the eight-person Board of Regents ever since.

Women had—and continue to have—virtually no representation at policy-making levels of the University. They are not represented on admissions committees by and large, which have continued to limit the numbers of women admitted.

And women have always been the vulnerable segment of the college population, as they have been of the working population.

In 1946, at the close of World War II, the number of freshman women admitted to the University was suddenly reduced by nearly a third, to allow admission of more veterans returning to college under the G. I. bill. That severe curtailment of women's admissions at Michigan—which continued from 1946 until 1952—no doubt repeated in universities throughout the United States at that time—had far-reaching effects on women's lives for the next decade and longer.

Because several hundred fewer women were admitted as undergraduates between 1946 and 1952, the proportion of women earning advanced degrees a few years later showed a marked decrease. While women had earned 1 in 6 Ph.D. degrees in 1920, they earned only 1 in 10 in 1956. Though the rising birth rate of the 1950's has generally been held accountable, more directly significant was the drastic reduction of women entering undergraduate studies in the late '40's and early '50's.

Not until the early 1960's did the downward trend begin to reverse itself. For the first time in decades new attention began to turn on the education of women, and on inequities in the legal and social structure that gave women essentially the status of a minority group.

The change was stimulated in part by renewed interest in intellectual quality and achievement. "Americans," writes William O'Neill, "became aware again of a vast, untapped reservoir of feminine ability—a point underlined by the Soviets, who in putting not only the first man but the first woman in space reminded us that a society that neglects the talents of half its population does so at its own peril."[6]

President Kennedy appointed the first Commission on the Status of Women in 1961.

To help release that "vast, untapped reservoir of feminine ability," the Center for Continuing Education of Women was founded at the University in 1964, one of the first such centers in the United States. Its primary job was to counsel women whose education had been interrupted and to help the University understand and respond to their special problems. Michigan alumnae provided half the funding fot the Center during its first three years of operation. By the end of the decade several thousand women had been encouraged to return to school or sometimes directly to employment.

In their attitude toward women students, the University had come full circle. Undergraduate life changed in important ways too. Special rules and regulations governing the lives of women students were abolished. Coed dormitories were introduced—or, one might say, coed living was re-introduced.

"The University," admitted the Reed Report of the Special Study Committee on Student Affairs that finally in 1962 abolished the office of Dean of Women, "has in fact held clearly different assumptions for men and women, the men being thought to be ready for great individual responsibility during their first year and almost full responsibility thereafter, and the women being assumed to need protection and regulation throughout their undergraduate years."[7]

In still another wav the women's movement appeared to have come full circle.

The feminist thrust of the nineteenth century in the United States had arisen directly out of the movement to abolish slavery. Out of the movement for civil rights for black people in the early 1960's came a new awareness among women of their own disadvantaged position in society. A whole new generation of young activists emerged, and a new women's liberation movement spread in a few years to every college campus and every major city in the country, focussing fresh attention on the need for ending discriminatory laws and practices.

What Happens to Women Scholars?

UNDERGRADUATE

16 % Women Undergraduates
Received LS&A Honors
(To 16% Men)

Grade Point Average of all
Woman Students is 3.01
(to 2.85 for Men)

GRADUATE

Only 37% Grad School Students
are Women (to 63% Men)

Only 19% Graduate-Professional
School Students are
Women (to 81% Men)

Life Patterns of American Women Today

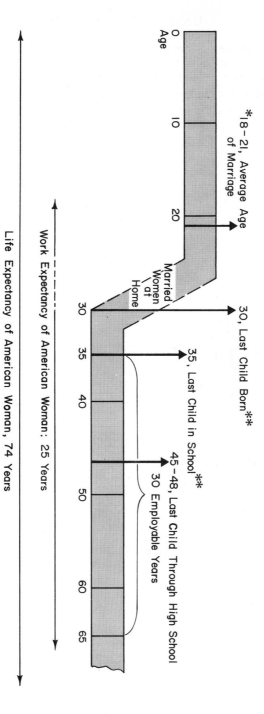

*18 – 21, Average Age of Marriage

30, Last Child Born**

35, Last Child in School**

45 – 48, Last Child Through High School

30 Employable Years

Married Women at Home

Work Expectancy of American Woman: 25 Years

Life Expectancy of American Woman, 74 Years

0 Age
10
20
30
35
40
50
60
65

* Trend Toward Later Marrying Age in Women
** Trend Toward Smaller Families Will Reduce This Age

Michigan and the University

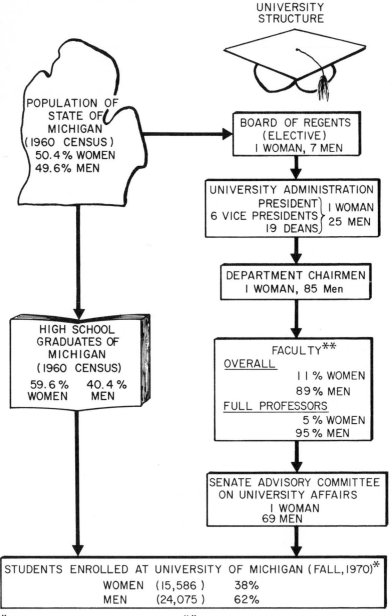

UNIVERSITY STRUCTURE

POPULATION OF STATE OF MICHIGAN (1960 CENSUS)
50.4% WOMEN
49.6% MEN

BOARD OF REGENTS (ELECTIVE)
I WOMAN, 7 MEN

UNIVERSITY ADMINISTRATION
PRESIDENT
6 VICE PRESIDENTS
19 DEANS
} I WOMAN
25 MEN

DEPARTMENT CHAIRMEN
I WOMAN, 85 Men

HIGH SCHOOL GRADUATES OF MICHIGAN (1960 CENSUS)
59.6% WOMEN   40.4% MEN

FACULTY**
OVERALL
11% WOMEN
89% MEN
FULL PROFESSORS
5% WOMEN
95% MEN

SENATE ADVISORY COMMITTEE ON UNIVERSITY AFFAIRS
I WOMAN
69 MEN

STUDENTS ENROLLED AT UNIVERSITY OF MICHIGAN (FALL, 1970)*
WOMEN   (15,586)   38%
MEN   (24,075)   62%

*Information from Office of Registrar   **Rank of Instructor and Above

15

The 1970's: A View from the Bell Tower

It will be equally difficult to show why every woman who desires and is qualified for the education provided in our universities should not as freely as any man have access to their privileges . . .
— President Angell, Report to the Regents, 1874

Discrimination in education is one of the most damaging injustices women suffer. It denies them equal education and equal employment opportunity, contributing to a second class self image.
— Report of the President's Task Force on Women's Rights and Responsibilities, 1970

And so—a full century after the first women gained the first reluctant admission to the University, where are we today? Are we visible at last, we women black and white? Have all doors opened to us as *persons*, human beings without regard to sex? Is the view of the campus finally a view through both eyes of the binoculars?

The proportion of women enrolled has not changed in 40 years. It lingers still at approximately 37 per cent, though women make up 50.4 per cent of the population of Michigan, and though more girls than boys graduate from high school. Admissions officers have cheerfully admitted over the years that they discriminate on the basis of sex, that more qualified girls than boys are refused admittance to the University. A recent study of 240 colleges and universities in the United States observed widespread discrimination against women and blacks in admissions procedures.[1]

And although women students maintain consistently a higher grade-point average than men—3.01 to 2.85—and share honors equally with men at the annual Honors Convocation—they are less apt than men to continue on to graduate education. Only 1 in 3 graduate students is a woman, only 1 in 5 scholars in doctoral programs is a woman. And although women have better over-all academic records as undergraduates, and tend to perform a bit better than men on the entrance examinations for professional schools, only 1 in 5 students in the graduate professional programs is a woman.

On the University faculty, some 80 years after Lucinda Hinsdale Stone made her plea for the appointment of women scholars and tried to raise single-handed $100,000 to pay them, and 80 years after the Board of Regents resolved to banish discrimination in faculty hiring on the basis of sex—women still make up only 11 per cent of the faculty (instructor and above), and only 5 per cent of full professors. Of that total the larger number are clustered in the traditionally feminine Schools of Nursing, Social Work, Education.

It appears that not only must women measure up on the academic scales men have established, they must actually excel men in those measurements. A survey of the hiring practices of department heads in colleges and universities showed that though they disavowed sex prejudice, in general they hired a woman only when she *excelled* all men applying for the post. And although a number of men without Ph.D.'s appear in the upper faculty ranks in the Literary College, there are no women without Ph.D.'s in comparable positions. Traditionally male-dominated departments, like faculty committees, exhibit typically a single token woman on their teaching staffs—if the department is especially lucky, a black woman, who can serve as a double token. As Caplow and McGee point out in their study of nation-wide academic hiring practices, [women] "are outside the prestige system entirely and for this reason are of no use to a department in future recruitment . . . Women scholars are not taken seriously and cannot look forward to a normal professional career."[2]

Thus the faculty remains by and large less a *community* of scholars than a *fraternity* of scholars.

Dean William Hays of the Literary College blames the low ratio

Bill Harris and Ellen Erlanger, Student Interest Coordinators, University Activities Program.—*Photo by Lee*

Gymnasium has changed since Eliza Mosher's day. Here a girl ballet artist practices on the high bar. (Photo by Lee.)

Mrs. Barbara Newell, special assistant to President Fleming, formerly Acting Vice-President for Student Affairs, was for a time the lone woman in top level university administration in any of the Big Ten colleges. Now there is none.

Mrs. Alison Myers, Executive Secretary of the Michigan Alumnae Council. Women graduates have raised over the years a half million dollars in scholarship funds.

Dr. Elizabeth Crosby, Professor Emeritus of Anatomy and Consultant in Neurosurgery, was the first woman professor in the Medical School, and the first woman to win the Distinguished Faculty Achievement Award in 1956.

The Child Care Action Group, supported by Women's Liberation groups on campus, maintains the Drop-in Day Care Center in Mary Markley Residence Hall. The Center cares for pre-school children of University students and employees. (Ann Arbor News Photo.)

Danute Miskinis was choreographer of a recent Musket Show. (Photo by Lee.)

Regent Gertrude Huebner, Phi Beta Kappa graduate, class of 1936, is the fourth woman to serve on the Board of Regents.

of women in doctoral programs on the "teacher-apprentice aspect of advanced graduate study and research. A man can give his full time to his learning role, a woman usually cannot."

Not only are women hired in fewer numbers, but they are paid less than men at the same rank on the faculty. The University of Michigan has not done a complete comparison of men's and women's salaries. However, a comparison of median salaries of women on the Literary College faculty with the median pay scale in the College shows that most women receive approximately 10 to 20 per cent below the median—the differential with men's salaries would be even higher. Studies of faculty salaries at other colleges exhibit the same disparity. A recent study at the University of Minnesota showed that women earn from 9 per cent to 32 per cent less than men for the same positions.

Bright young women students aspiring to a career of research and teaching can find few models, and they receive little encouragement from what they actually see of the woman scholar's life.

The University experience is, of course, only one chapter in the life of a woman or a man—but it happens to be a critical one.

When we begin to draw the profile of the woman student today, to compare her with the student of Madelon Stockwell's time, it appears that her early socialization is not too different from that of a hundred years ago.

While we still know too little about what constitute innate sex differences, we are learning a great deal about the effects of early conditioning on both girls and boys.

Professors Elizabeth Douvan and Judith Bardwick of the Psychology Department note that "sex differences in infancy and childhood are enlarged through socialization," and point to the far greater difficulty encountered by the adolescent girl in achieving a sense of independence and self-identity in the face of society's tendency to foster psychological dependency and to direct her to seek identity through a husband. They add: "We know it is destructive to feelings of esteem to know that you are capable and to be aware that you are not utilizing much of your potential."[3]

Dr. Matina Horner, now at Harvard University, whose doctoral thesis at Michigan was written on "Sex Differences in Achievement Motivation and Performance in Competitive and Non-Competitive Situations," (1968) pinpointed, described and documented "fear of success" as a psychological barrier to achievement in women. She declares:

> Unfortunately in American society, even today, feminin-
> ity and competitive achievement continue to be viewed
> as two desirable but mutually exclusive ends . . . Thus
> the active pursuit of success is hindered and the actual
> level of performance attained by many otherwise
> achievement-motivated and able young women does not
> reflect their true abilities . . . This unfulfillment does not
> occur without a price, a price paid in feelings of frus-
> tration, hostility, aggression, bitterness and confusion.[4]

Because of early training to downgrade their own intellectual
ability and achievement, most young women doubtless need *additional* support and encouragement at the college level. Instead,
they usually receive less encouragement than men students,
especially if they hope to enter any except fields long deemed
"feminine" and therefore appropriate—such fields as teaching,
nursing, social work, librarianship. To continue on to graduate
work, especially in any of the male-dominated fields or professions,
women students must not only be as well-motivated, but better-
motivated than their fellow male students.

Noel Anketell Kramer, senior law student, member of the Law
Review, and president of Kappa Beta Pi, Women Lawyers' Club,
describes the situation for women students in the Law School
where they make up only 7 per cent of the enrollment:

> The woman student is caught on the horns of a dilemma.
> If she is quiet and does not assert herself in class, she is
> called passive and this supposedly proves she will never
> make a good lawyer. On the other hand, those of us who
> are more assertive are labelled aggressive, castrating
> females, who will do anything to get ahead. Somewhere
> in this process the woman law student begins to ques-
> tion her femininity and to wonder if perhaps there is not
> indeed something wrong with her.[5]

Interestingly enough, while the white girl at the pre-college level
is still taught to look to marriage as her principal goal in life, the
black girl has higher academic aspirations, and does not center her
plans around being a housewife-sans-other-identity. Richard A.
English, Lecturer in Social Work, has recently completed a revealing study of the attitudes toward higher education of black and
white boys and girls in inner city low-income and outer-city middle-
income populations of Detroit. He found his own conclusions

startling: "The chief differences in educational aspirations," he says, "are not along race, as I'd expected, but along sex lines." The groups with the highest educational aspirations were black females, the group with the lowest, white females. "The highest drop-out rate for the inner-city schools, white and black," says English, "was among white females."

He continues, "Black females tend to look more like males in terms of aspirations than white females . . . The biggest proportion wanting to be housewives was among white women. In 1963 the mothers had been interviewed, and the black mothers wanted their girls to go to college, the opposite of whites . . . Females' sights are lowered by what happens to them in schools, counselors who put them into tracks in sixth grade."[6]

Black women in the University—approximately 367 at the last count—make up about 46 per cent of the black student population—numerically closer to sex parity than the white student body.

According to Dr. Nellie Varner, Assistant Professor of Political Science, and one of the few black women on the University faculty, "There is no question that blacks and women are discriminated against; black women face double discrimination." She adds thoughtfully: "Race barriers are falling more easily than sex."[7]

One of the most significant changes in the profile of the woman student today over a hundred years ago is in wide diversity of age. Even in Madelon Stockwell's day women students were apt to be from two to five years older than their male counterparts. But today the ages of women students on campus range from 16 to 70, with more than 4000 twenty-five and over.

Still another change is the fact that today's student, male or female, may be married. One in 10 undergraduate women students is married; nearly one-half on the graduate level are married.

An unknown quantity is the student wife not enrolled in the University, the woman student who has married and dropped out, perhaps for financial reasons—to help earn her husband's way through college or a graduate degree—or to have a baby. Michigan has never made a study of student wives, but Helen B. Schleman, former dean of women at Purdue, where such a study was made, believes that "there are many, many more married men students on our campuses, whose nonstudent wives are with them, than there are married women students. For the most part, husbands are in school, but their wives are not."[8]

Coed dormitories (like this one, Mosher-Jordan) are not really new. For the first 25 years, Michigan women had no special rules, lived in mixed rooming houses in town. (Photo by Lee.)

Today's women activists continue a long tradition of participation in social causes that began with the women abolitionists more than a century ago. (Photo by Davis.)

Mary Lanson, JoAnne Battie, exchange students from Tuskegee Institute in Alabama. In 1878 the first black woman, Virginia Watts, enrolled at Michigan, graduated from Medical School. Today nearly 400 black women study in the University—and a much larger enrollment is sought. (University News Service.)

Today's staff of the *Michigan Daily*. Gertrude Buck, '94, first woman to serve on the *Daily* staff, became associate editor, earned four degrees at Michigan, later taught at Vassar. (Photo by Lee.)

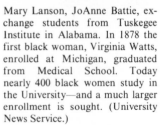

Today's women students, like the first admitted, rank high in scholarship, carry off more than their proportion of academic honors. Though women still face prejudice in many areas of the University, and later in professional life, some are enrolled in virtually every department and school of the University. (Photos by Davis, lower right by Lee.)

A DANGEROUS EXPERIMENT

The Center for Continuing Education of Women is helping this group by making available classes that are the full credit equivalent of the usual daytime courses at evening hours when working wives and young mothers can attend—and with others like themselves. Reaching out to these women who are at the busiest period of their lives, and holding the door open to higher education while they are on the University's doorstep, is a positive action of enormous importance.

The University has had to grow more elastic in the last few years to encompass its increasingly diverse student body.

Part-time study, on both undergraduate and graduate levels, permits working students to pursue their studies; it also permits women with family responsibilities to continue their educations. Not all professional schools have yet modified their regulations to include the part-time student, but if they do, the next few years may see increasing numbers of women and men studying medicine and law while they work or maintain families.

Additional financial aid for the returning woman student—whose educational expenses are usually at the very bottom of family budget priorities—is a crucial need. When the Center for Continuing Education of Women offered six $1500 merit fellowships for returning women in 1970, 193 women applied—most of them able, some highly gifted women—and nearly all facing financial difficulty in continuing their studies. Vitally needed are still larger fellowships to enable talented women black and white who are heads of families to complete their educational goals. In addition to the six merit fellowships, the Center gives emergency grants that often spell the difference between completing a degree or leaving college—sometimes steps in to pay for such a special expense as photographs to accompany a doctoral dissertation.

The returning woman student, whose education has been interrupted, is typically—like the first women students whose educational privileges had been so hard-won—highly motivated, hardworking, and high-achieving. These women are in college because they have a definite aim; they are the kind of "volunteer students" whom President Kingman Brewster of Yale hopes will make up the student population of future campuses.

Nobody knows, of course, what will be the accepted life pattern of women in the next half century—nor of men either, for that matter.

But the employment trend for women is definitely upward, and the more education a woman has, the greater are the chances that she is now—or will be—employed for a large part of her life. In 1968 71 per cent of women with 5 years or more of college were in the labor market, and estimates are that by 1980 75 per cent of all women college graduates will be employed. Although the median income earned by women remains substantially below that of men— and unhappily that earnings gap is widening—nevertheless, a woman's earning power is directly correlated with the amount of education she has.

The employment pattern for college-trained women of the present generation has been to work until the birth of a child, to drop out for a few years until the youngest child is in school or through school, then return either for additional education or directly into part- or full-time employment. Probably the in-out-in pattern will continue for many educated women. But the "out" part in women's life pattern is certain to be abbreviated with the trend toward smaller families and better child-care facilities.

Increasingly, younger women appear to be looking ahead to an uninterrupted career running parallel with marriage. High-achieving senior women, members of Mortar Board Honor Society, surveyed as to their plans, replied nearly without exception that they planned to continue through graduate or professional schools, and to pursue a career, most think now, along with eventual marriage. The early marriage trend of a few years ago appears to be losing momentum, and this factor too will affect women's lives and educational fulfillment.

Probably the married professional woman will still have to be, like her counterpart today, something of a Renaissance human being, a *femmina universale,* handling skillfully all the various components of her life.

As the anonymous woman historian interviewed by the author of *The Woman Doctorate in America* remarks of marriage:

> Perhaps women will use their talents better when they fully realize that "to get married and live happily ever after" is not a goal that is directly achievable; it is more likely to be the by-product of an interesting and productive life.[9]

Women by and large—whether by nature or by social rearing— are versatile, adaptable creatures. They've had to be. For their first hundred years at Michigan they have fit themselves amiably—or as amiably as possible—into a structure not at all tailored to their needs. There are hopeful signs for the 1970's that the old feudal structure of the university—which has made it primarily a profess-ional training school for young white males aged 19 to 22—has changed and is continuing to change. The pigeonhole concept of higher education as belonging exclusively to a brief segment of any-one's chronological life has certainly changed. Already there is a more flexible pattern of life emerging within the university.

Young women and men are rejecting the stereotyped male and female sex roles, "which", say Professors Bardwick and Douvan, "are costly because they push men and women into limited slots solely on the basis of sex."[9] And if young people are rejecting those stereotypes, so are many of their elders—a fact the young have not always noticed. The phenomenon of the mother in classes at the University (her numbers have not yet been counted, but one hopes they will be)—the mother of 10 children pursuing her studies in Medical School, the mother of 5 driving a school bus to pay her tuition costs—are as far from a sex stereotype (aproned mother in the kitchen) as the young student couple dividing household chores so both can complete their degrees. According to Bardwick and Douvan: "Today college students seem to have a better aware-ness than we did of the consequences of role choice and they seem to be evolving a goal in which men are more nurturant than they were, while females are freer to participate professionally with-out endangering the esteem of the male."[10]

It will be comparatively easy for the University—which is, in the end, all of us, students, staff, graduates, parents of children for whose education the University was created—it will be comparatively easy for the University to banish overt discrimination in admissions, in hiring practices, in salaries. Self-examination and new guidelines are obviously of prime importance. Equally important is the kind of affirmative action program now widely used to recruit students and faculty from minority groups—to find and actively encourage able women for graduate work, for professional schools, for the faculty.

But even more we need a different, much broader vision of hu-man fulfillment, female as well as male. We need more flexible yardsticks for measuring accomplishment than the ones of a cen-tury ago. We need a different view of a university's possibilities—

and it must be a vision through the eyes and brains of women as well as men, of black as well as white.

For if a society is to change itself for the better without violence, if it is to measure its success no longer in terms of Gross National Product but of fulfilling human needs, where can it turn for its lessons if not to a great university?

Erik Erikson, among others, thinks:

> There will be many difficulties in a new joint adjustment of the sexes to changing conditions, but they do not justify prejudices which keep half of mankind from participating in planning and decision-making, especially at a time when the other half, by its competitive escalation and acceleration of technological progress has brought us and our children to the gigantic brink on which we live, with all our affluence.

Notes

Note on bibliographical sources. The Michigan Historical Collection (abbreviated below as MHC) is, of course, the most important source for materials dealing with University of Michigan history. The Alumni Records Office of the University has provided valuable material on individual alumnae. Mrs. Edna French was kind enough to lend her private collection of University of Michigan memorabilia.

1. New Student on Campus

1. Belle McArthur Perry, *Lucinda Hinsdale Stone* (Detroit, Blinn Publishing Company, 1902), p. 115.

2. Marie Louise Walker, "Early Days of Coeducation," *The Inlander,* (April, 1896), p. 277.

3. *Ypsilanti Sentinel,* (January 1870,) Willard Scrapbooks, MHC.

4. Orlando Stephenson, Ann Arbor, The First Hundred Years (Ann Arbor, Chamber of Commerce, 1927),p. 267.

5. Elizabeth Gaspar Brown, "The Initial Admission of Negro Students to the University of Michigan," *Michigan Quarterly Review,* Vol. II, No. 1, (Winter, 1963).

6. Perry, p. 117.

7. Elizabeth Gaspar Brown, "Memorandum on the Mississippi Woman's Law of 1839," *Michigan Law Review,* (1944), and Karolena M. Fox, "History of the Equal Suffrage Movement in Michigan," *Michigan History Magazine,* Vol. 2 (1918), p. 92ff.

2. Before 1870: Women and History

1. Dorothy Gies, "Some Early Ladies of the Book Trade," *Publishers Weekly,* (Oct. 5, 1940).

2. Erik Erikson, *Young Man Luther* (New York, W. W. Norton, 1962), p. 71.

3. Florence M. Smith, *Mary Astell* (New York, Columbia University Press, 1916), pp. 42-43.

4. Mary R. Beard, *Woman as Force in History* (New York, Macmillan Co., 1946), p. 79.

5. Mary Wollstonecraft, *A Vindication of the Rights of Woman* (New York, W. W. Norton & Co., 1967), p. ii.

6. L. H. Butterfield, *Editor, Adams Family Correspondence* (Cambridge, Harvard University Press, 1963), I, p. 370; I, p. 382; II, p. 94; II, p. 109.

7. James Milnor, "On Female Education," in *Portfolio, A Monthly Miscellany,* Vol. 1, No. 5, (Philadelphia, 1809).

8. Gunnar Myrdal, *An American Dilemma, Vol. 2: The Negro Social Structure* (New York, McGraw Hill Book Co., 1964), Appendix 5, p. 1073 ff.

9. Aileen Kraditor, *Up from the Pedestal: Selected Writings in the History of American Feminism* (Chicago, Quadrangle Books, 1968), p. 62.

10. Kraditor, p. 51.

11. Kraditor, p. 54.

12. Kraditor, p. 185.

13. Kraditor, p. 190.

3. The Dangerous Experiment Begins

1. *Michigan Journal of Education,* Vol. II, (May 1855), p. 129.

2. Erastus O. Haven, *Autobiography* (New York, Phillips & Hunt, 1883), p. 110.

3. *Michigan Journal of Education,* II, p. 136.

4. *Ibid.,* p. 137.

5. *Ibid.,* p. 137.

6. *Ibid.,* p. 139.

7. *Proceedings of the University of Michigan Board of Regents, 1837-1864.*

8. *Detroit Free Press,* June 24, 1858.

9. Charles M. Perry, *Henry Philip Tappan* (Ann Arbor, University of Michigan Press, 1933), p. 362.

10. *Regents Proceedings,* June 24, 1858, p. 743.

11. *Ibid.,* September, 1858, Appendix B, "Report on the Admission of Females," p. 782.

12. *Detroit Free Press,* Oct. 2, 1858.

13. *Regents Proceedings,* p. 795.

14. *Ibid.,* June, 1859, p. 853.

15. Mary Elizabeth Massey, *Bonnet Brigades* (New York, Alfred A. Knopf, 1966), p. 160.

16. Obituary clippings furnished by Duluth Public Library Reference Department.

17. Perry, *Lucinda Stone,* p. 15 ff.

18. L. H. Stone, "History of Coeducation in the University of Michigan," *Michigan Pioneer and Historical Collections,* XVIII, p. 412 ff.

19. Alexander Winchell Diary, MHC.

20. Alexander Winchell, Miscellaneous Papers, MHC. Also, "Woman: Her Actual Place and Her Rightful Place," Mary Jo Pugh, *Editor,* in *Chronicle of the Historical Society of Michigan,* Vol. 6, No. 3, (1970), p. 17 ff.

NOTES

21. Alice Boise Wood, "How Michigan University was Opened to Women," *The Inlander* (April, 1896), p. 273.

22. *The Chronicle* (May 30, 1868), Vol. II, No. 34, p. 4.

23. *Proceedings of the Board of Regents of the University of Michigan, January 1864 to January 1870,* April 19, 1867, p. 200.

24. Mabel Newcomer, *A Century of Higher Education for Women* (New York, Harper & Brothers, 1959), p. 26.

25. *Regents Proceedings,* April 10, 1867, p. 200.

26. "Report of the President to the Board of Regents," *Regents Proceedings,* Sept. 24, 1867, p. 233.

27. *Regents Proceedings,* January 5, 1870, p. 2.

28. Willard Scrapbooks, MHC.

4. Pioneer Women at Michigan University

1. Olive San Louie Anderson, *An American Girl and her Four Years in a Boys' College* (New York, D. Appleton and Co., 1878), p. 52.

2. Caroline Hubbard Kleinstueck, "Four Years in a Boys' College," *Michigan Alumnus,* Vol. 32 (January, 1926) p. 285.

3. *The Chronicle,* February 12, 1870.

4. Letter of June 5, 1871, Thomas McIntyre Cooley Correspondence, 1862-1871, MHC.

5. *Michigan Argus,* January 6, 1870, Willard Scrapbooks, MHC.

5. First Women in Medicine

1. Florence Woolsey Hazzard, "Heart of the Oak: The Story of Eliza Mosher," unpublished biography, MHC.

2. "Memorial on Female Medical Education," March 25, 1870, in Papers of Board of Regents, 1867-1898 and undated, including communications 1869-1870 dealing with the admission of women to the Medical School, MHC.

3. *Ibid.,* "Report of Committee of the Medical Department," n.d.

4. *Ibid.,* "Second Report of the Department of Medicine and Surgery," July 26, 1870.

5. *Ibid.,* "Report of A. Sager, Dean of the Medical School, 1871."

6. Women and President Angell

1. *Oxford Dictionary* cites E. H. Clarke's *Sex In Education* (1874) for one of the earliest uses of the word.

2. W. Le Conte Stevens, "The Admission of Women to Universities," (1883), quoted in James L. Miller, "The Admission of Women to the Universities," *Michigan Quarterly Review* (Summer, 1962), Vol. 1, No. 3, p. 184.

3. Mabel A. Cosby, "Women at Michigan," unpublished term paper in History of Education, MHC, n.d., p. 11.

4. Report of President Angell to the Board of Regents, June 1872 in *Proceeding of the Board of Regents of the University of Michigan from January 1870 to January 1876.*

5. Report of President Angell to the Board of Regents, October 9, 1874.

6. George Herbert Palmer, *The Life of Alice Freeman Palmer* (Boston, Houghton Mifflin Co., 1908), p. 44.

7. James Burrill Angell, "On Coeducation," unpublished paper, n.d., in Angell Papers, Box 36, II-15 (MHC).

8. Winchell Scrapbooks, MHC, n.d., prob. 1867.

9. James Burrill Angell, "Report on Coeducation," *Pennsylvania School Journal,* (1881), quoted in Thomas Woody, *A History of Women's Education in the United States* (New York, Science Press, 1929), II, p. 246.

10. Howard H. Peckham, *The Making of the University of Michigan* (Ann Arbor, University of Michigan Press, 1967), p. 61.

11. Palmer, p. 64.

7. First Novel about the University

1. Anderson, *An American Girl,* p. 33 ff.

8. Dr. Clarke's Sex-and-Health Bogey

1. William L. O'Neill, *Everyone Was Brave—The Rise and Fall of Feminism in America* (Chicago, Quadrangle Books, 1969), p. 80.

2. Angell, Paper on "Coeducation", *op. cit.*

3. G. Stanley Hall, *Adolescence* (New York, D. Appleton and Company, 1904), II, p. 569; Clarke, p. 149.

4. Edward H. Clarke, *Sex in Education or A Fair Chance for Girls* (Boston, James R. Osgood and Company, 1875), p. 47.

5. Clarke, p. 21.

6. Clarke, p. 178.

7. Clarke, p. 29.

8. Clarke, p. 83.

9. Clarke, p. 86.

10. Clarke, p. 127.

11. Clarke, p. 116.

12. Clarke, p. 63.

13. Anderson, p. 96.

14. Anderson, p. 102.

15. Anderson, p. 97.

16. Clarke, p. 23.

17. Anderson, p. 98.

18. Woody II, p. 246.

19. Woody, II, p. 277.

20. Hall, II, p. 639.

NOTES

9. 1896: Women Get a Dean

1. Octavia Williams Bates, "Short History of the Movement for a Women's Building at the University of Michigan," *The Inlander,* (April, 1896), p. 260.

2. *Ibid.,* p. 261.

3. Miller, *op. cit.,* p. 185.

4. *The Chronicle,* Vol. V, No. V, (Nov. 29, 1873), p. 52-53.

5. Ruth B. Bordin, "Levi Lewis Barbour," *Michigan Quarterly Review,* (Winter, 1963), p. 38.

6. Florence Woolsey Hazzard, "Heart of Oak: The Story of Eliza Mosher," unpublished biography, MHC. Nearly all the material on Eliza Mosher in Chapter 9 comes from this excellent 2-volume typescript. It has not been paginated.

7. Sara Spencer Brown, "Dr. Eliza M. Mosher," *The Inlander,* (April, 1896), p. 272.

8. Hazzard, "Eliza Mosher."

10. How the First Graduates Used Their Education

1. Woody, II, p. 261.

2. *Regents Proceedings,* September 1858, Appendix B., p. 787.

3. Alumni Records, file on Annie Peck.

4. *Ibid.*

5. James Burrill Angell, "Review of *The Life of Alice Freeman Palmer,*" *Michigan Alumnus,* (June 1908), pp. 402-3.

6. Palmer, p. 51.

7. Florence Hazzard, "Alice Freeman Palmer," unpublished biographical sketch, MHC, p. 6.

8. Hazzard, "Eliza Mosher."

9. Louise Fargo Brown, *Apostle of Democracy, The Life of Lucy Maynard Salmon* (New York, Harper & Brothers, 1943), p. 93.

10. *Ibid.,* p. 98.

11. *U. of M. Daily,* December 16, 1899.

12. James Burrill Angell, *N.E.A. Proceedings,* (1904), quoted in Woody, II, p. 301.

13. Palmer, p. 52.

14. *Ibid.*

15. Hazzard, "Alice Freeman Palmer," p. 11.

16. Hazzard, "Eliza Mosher."

17. Quoted in Hall, *Adolescence,* II, p. 582.

18. James Rowland Angell, "Some Reflections upon the Reaction from Coeducation," in *Popular Science Monthly,* Vol. LXII, (November, 1902), p. 21.

11. Of Clubs and Women Professors

1. Perry, *Lucinda Stone*, p. 161.

2. Lucinda Hinsdale Stone to President James Burrill Angell, July 26, 1890, Angell Papers, Box 13, No. 6, MHC.

3. Lucinda Hinsdale Stone, "An Appeal to the Regents," reprinted in "History of Co-Education in the University of Michigan," *Michigan Pioneer and Historical Collections* (Lansing, 1892), Vol. XVIII, p. 415.

4. Carol Lopate, *Women in Medicine* (Baltimore, Johns Hopkins Press, 1968), p. 14.

5. *Regents Proceedings,* June 25, 1894, p. 293.

6. Symposium, "The Admission of Women to the Faculty of the University," in *The Castalian,* (1896), Collection of Mrs. Leslie French, p. 43 ff.

7. Minutes of Michigan Alumnae Council Executive Committee.

8. Stone, "An Appeal to the Regents," p. 417.

12. Dr. Alice Hamilton and the "Dangerous Trades"

1. Madeleine P. Grant, *Alice Hamilton* (New York, Abelard-Schuman, 1967), p. 124.

2. Alice Hamilton, *Exploring the Dangerous Trades* (Boston, Little Brown and Company, 1943), p. 121.

3. *Ibid.,* p. 40, 41.

4. *Ibid.,* pp. 44, 46.

5. Grant, p. 46.

6. Jane Addams, "Woman's Conscience and Social Amelioration," in *The Social Application of Religion* (Cincinnati, Jennings & Graham, 1908), p. 41.

7. Hamilton, p. 128.

8. O'Neill, *Everyone Was Brave,* p. 169.

9. Grant, p. 106. The plan for "continuous mediation" was first proposed by Julia G. Wales, of the University of Wisconsin.

10. Hamilton, p. 236.

11. Grant, p. 138.

13. Two Steps Back in the 1900's

1. Woody, II, p. 272.

2. James Rowland Angell, "Some Reflections upon the Reaction from Coeducation," *Popular Science Monthly,* (November, 1902) p. 5.

3. Phi Beta Kappa, Alpha Chapter of Michigan, Minutes 1907-1930.

4. Albert P. Jacobs, "A Consequence of Co-Education," in *The Inlander,* Vol. II, (December, 1891).

5. Theodore Roosevelt, "Race Decadence," *The Outlook,* (April 8, 1911), p. 765. Roosevelt even considered three-child marriages "sterile marriages," on the ground that one extra child did not allow for the possibility of death. He did not, however, blame the emancipation of women for the declining

NOTES

birth rate. See also David Kennedy, *Birth Control in America* (New Haven, Yale University Press, 1970), p. 42.

6. Herbert Spencer, *Principles of Biology,* II, p. 512.

7. G. Stanley Hall, *N.E.A. Proceedings, 1903,* quoted in Woody, II, p. 274.

8. G. Stanley Hall, *Adolescence,* II, p. 614.

9. Helen Walker Puner, *Freud: His Life and His Mind* (New York, Howell, Soskin, 1947), p. 166.

10. James Rowland Angell, *op. cit.,* p. 21.

11. Brown, *op. cit.,* p. 101.

12. *School Journal,* LXXIII, 361, quoted in Woody, II, 281.

13. Woody, II, p. 291.

14. *Ibid.,* p. 293.

15. *Ibid.,* p. 294.

16. Peckham, p. 165.

14. Revolution in Slow Motion

1. Leo Kanowitz, *Women and the Law.* (Albuquerque, University of New Mexico Press, 1969).

2. Grant Allen, "Plain Words on the Woman Question," quoted in Hall, *Adolescence,* II, p. 576.

3. *Michigan Daily,* May 11, 1920.

4. Quoted by Marjorie Lansing in "Sex Differences in Political Participation," Doctoral Dissertation, University of Michigan Department of Political Science, 1970, p. 118.

5. Mabel Newcomer, *A Century of Higher Education for American Women* (New York, Harper & Brothers, 1959) p. 129.

6. O'Neill, *op. cit.,* p. 339.

7. Report of the Special Study Committee for the Office of Student Affairs, February, 1962.

15. The 1970's: A View from the Bell Tower

1. *Chronicle of Higher Education,* May 11, 1970.

2. Theodore Caplow and Reece J. McGee, *The Academic Marketplace* (New York, Basic Books, 1958), pp. 111-112.

3. Judith M. Bardwick and Elizabeth Douvan, "Ambivalence in Women and its Socialization," in *51%—The Case for Women's Liberation,* Barbara Moran and Vivian Gornick, *Eds.,* (New York, Basic Books, to be published Spring, 1971.)

4. Matina Horner, Research Report given at C.C.E.W. Symposium, "Toward a New Psychology of Women," University of Michigan, October 14, 1970.

5. Noel Anketell Kramer, Paper given at Round Table Discussion, "The Case of the Woman Graduate Student," C.C.E.W. Symposium, University of Michigan, October 14, 1970.

6. Richard A. English, Lecturer in Social Work, Report on his research findings given in interview, July 31, 1970.

7. Nellie Varner, Assistant Professor of Political Science, in an interview, April 22, 1970.

8. Helen B. Schleman, former Dean of Women at Purdue, "Educational Planning for Wives of Men Students," in *Journal of National Association of Deans and Counsellors,* (Fall, 1969), p. 23.

9. Helen Astin, *The Woman Doctorate in America* (New York, Russell Sage Foundation, 1969), p. 120.

10. Bardwick and Douvan, *op. cit.*

11. *Ibid.*

ABOUT THE PICTURES

All early pictures are from the archives of the Michigan Historical Collections except three. The photograph of Olive San Louie Anderson is from the Department of Rare Books and Special Collections, that of Virginia Watts from the archives of the Medical School, and that of Annie Peck from the Alumni Records Office. The Daumier prints in the Bluestocking Series are from private collections.

Contemporary photographs are as indicated by Richard Lee, and others; the Sesqui-Centennial pictures are by Philip C. Davis, Professor of Art.

Picture layout by Paul Brown.

Charts by Harry J. Wilsher.

Index

INDEX